KODAK CREATIVE PHOTOGRAPHY

Editor-in-Chief
Jack Tresidder

Art Director
Mel Petersen

Series Editor
John Roberts

Editorial Assistant
Margaret Little

Designers
Robert Lamb
Lisa Tai

Production
Peter Phillips
Jean Rigby

Editors
Ian Chilvers
Lucy Lidell
Joss Pearson
Richard Platt

Picture Researchers
Brigitte Arora
Nicky Hughes

Co-ordinating Editors for Kodak
Kenneth T. Lassiter
Kenneth R. Oberg
Jacalyn R. Salitan

Consulting Photographer
Michael Freeman

Created and designed, in association with Kodak, by Mitchell Beazley
an imprint of
Reed Consumer Books Limited
Michelin House
81 Fulham Road
London SW3 6RB
and Auckland, Melbourne, Singapore and Toronto

Copyright © 1983 Kodak Limited, Mitchell Beazley International Limited,
Salvat Editores, S.A.

This edition first published in 1993 by
Chancellor Press
an imprint of
Reed Consumer Books Limited

ISBN 1 85152 437 1

Produced by Mandarin Offset
Printed in China

Part 2   The Magic of Colour

THE KEY TO PHOTOGRAPHY

The best photographs are simple. They convey a message directly and vividly – whether the joy of a family reunion or the splendour of a canyon lit by the evening sky. This same simplicity often applies to the way they are taken. Creative photographers develop the ability to take interesting pictures by the most straightforward means. Modern cameras and films, efficient and easy to use, have greatly reduced difficulties in assessing exposure and other such technical problems – freeing the photographer's eye and imagination. The aim of this book is to show that anyone, from the novice to experienced – and often frustrated – amateur, can master the simple techniques and clear creative principles that will transform their photography.

The pictures on the following nine pages include striking images that any photographer would be proud to take. But in spite of their high quality, none involved difficult techniques, and indeed several were taken by amateurs. The key to the success of these pictures is that each concentrates on a single uncomplicated idea. A similar portfolio of pictures introduces Part Two of the book, which focuses on colour photography as a major subject in its own right.

The pure white facade of a colonial weatherboard house demonstrates that simple images are often the strongest. The photographer crouched low and tilted his camera to exclude every distraction and reduce the scene to two elements – blue sky and gleaming house.

The clean drama of a near-horizontal water-skier against a wall of spray and an unexpectedly calm reflection combine in a remarkable action shot. This picture was taken from the rear of the towing boat, using a telephoto lens and a fast shutter speed. The impact of the image is heightened by its basic clarity and isolation from any visual clutter – the skier almost filling the width of the frame and snapped just as he banks over to round the buoy, leaving clear water between him and the speeding boat.

Rainy weather, *often thought unsuitable for photography, creates some of the most interesting photographic opportunities. Amateur Luis Huesco took advantage of it when he was on a tour of a Spanish museum. Through a half-open door, he noticed the chance presented by two children playing alone in a drenched courtyard. In spite of their rushing figures, the scene seems charged with an eerie stillness, an effect created by the weather's grey mood in the symmetrical setting.*

The inspired pattern of this unusual image came from the photographer's simple realization that a plaything such as a badminton shuttlecock can cast fascinating shadows when placed in front of a strong light source. By mating a pair of shuttlecocks in the light of a slide projector, the delicate ribbed wings of a shadow-insect were created.

The sparkle of a smile
and the bright red of a sun
hat in the picture above
lend the simplest of portraits
an infectious gaiety. The
photographer moved in close
to frame the girl against the
plain white wall and intensify
the impact of the peaked cap
above her glowing face.

The yellow rain hat pulled
over the child's face makes a
telling portrait that needed
only an open response to the
sudden opportunity. Many
photographers would have
waited, or asked the boy to
lift the hat up again for a
clear view, missing the
drama of the invisible face.

Blurred water – achieved by a slow shutter speed – in this sombre landscape has smoothed out the one active element of the scene and turned the picture into a hauntingly beautiful still-life. The strange effect was surprisingly easy to create, needing no more than a time exposure of a few seconds.

A majestic baboon, *isolated by a telephoto lens, displays the soft colours and strongly defined patterns of his facial markings. Like many good animal shots, this is not an exotic wildlife picture: the photographer spotted the baboon in the shady doorway of its zoo den, and closed in.*

YOU, THE PHOTOGRAPHER

Good photographs come from developing an eye for a picture – not from using banks of powerful studio lights, whirring motor-drives or two-foot-long telephoto lenses. Success requires no more than the ability to make the essential creative leap from what you see to what will work as a photographic image. The secret of doing this is to train the eye to see images that will give pleasure when they are taken out of the complex, confused and constantly shifting world and made into photographs isolated by their frames.

Experienced photographers become adept at identifying interesting images largely because they spend a great deal of time looking through the viewfinders of their cameras. Anyone can learn to see pictures in the same way. Look through the viewfinder frequently, even when you do not intend to take a picture. Concentrate on what you can actually see in the frame and how the shapes or colours there work together. You can practise this way of seeing even when you do not have a camera with you – remember the old artist's trick of holding the hands up as a frame? This creative and imaginative process is at the heart of photography, and the pictures on the following pages emphasize how much effective images depend on vision itself.

The viewfinder is your photographic link with the world in front of the camera. Here, the edges of its frame isolate four silhouetted figures from the bustle of a city park. The picture is compelling because the photographer used the camera's special eye to select the right image at the right moment.

Seeing pictures

Distant details, such as the woman walking her dog, may attract the eye, but are not clearly visible. However, with a telephoto lens, the camera can close in on such images.

To begin seeing as the camera sees, you need to recognize its basic powers – and limitations. First, consider the similarities between the camera and the eye. Both use a lens to focus an image on a surface that is sensitive to light. And a camera has ways of controlling the intensity of the incoming light, much as the pupil of the eye does. But, while these parallels are interesting, the differences are actually more relevant when you try to take pictures. In particular, the eye has vastly greater flexibility, working automatically in a way that the most advanced electronic camera cannot emulate.

Because you have two eyes, your brain receives two views of any subject from slightly different angles. Fused together into a single image, they form a picture that gives you a greater sense of depth than any photograph could provide. Moreover, the camera takes in the whole scene with uncritical interest, whereas your eyes concentrate on the parts of the scene you find most interesting.

The focus of the eye can change so swiftly from near to far objects that all appear equally in focus.

A boy playing may move too fast for the eye to capture his actions. But the camera can freeze every detail – even the ball in mid-air.

The eye
The remarkable versatility of human vision stems from the close link between the eye and the brain. Without our being consciously aware of the process, the brain controls the eye as it rapidly scans a scene to build up a complete picture, focusing on various details and adjusting to differing light levels. At the same time, the brain interprets the information received, making sense, for example, of the changes in scale between objects as they appear to diminish in size with distance. Vision extends through a full 160°, compared with the 45° view of a normal camera lens.

Images from the real world
Photographs may look like
the real world – but do not
duplicate the eye's view,
here represented by a hand-
tinted, retouched image.
This scene in a park around
a mansion includes several
photographic subjects, some
of which are reproduced in
the insets. Each inset picture
captures an image different
from one the eye would see.

The camera, however, can focus only a part of the
scene in one picture. The eye is also a great deal
more flexible in handling extreme contrasts in the
light level. Within the same scene, we can distinguish details of objects in deep shadow and in
bright sunlight in a way that is denied to the camera.

On the other hand, the camera has certain powers
that are beyond those of the eye. By framing a small
part of the world and thus engaging our attention,
a photograph can make us see things that might
otherwise go unnoticed. And the camera's ability to
freeze motion can reveal details of moving objects
not always visible to the naked eye.

Perhaps the most essential of all these things to
remember is that your eye can notice instanta-
neously what interests you in a scene and ignore the
rest, shifting attention constantly from the whole to
the smallest detail in a changing stream. The camera,
by contrast, fixes the whole scene in the viewfinder
at the moment you press the shutter. You must
provide the discrimination by so directing the
camera that worthwhile images are selected.

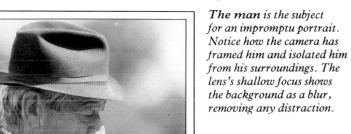

*The man is the subject
for an impromptu portrait.
Notice how the camera has
framed him and isolated him
from his surroundings. The
lens's shallow focus shows
the background as a blur,
removing any distraction.*

The camera
The camera's relative lack of flexibility means that
you must operate it carefully to record effective
images. First, focus must be adjusted for the subject
to appear sharp. The amount of light allowed to fall
on the film must also be just right – and even then
the contrast between light and dark areas in a scene
may be too great for detail to show in both. On the
other hand, the camera records an image fixed in time,
allowing us to keep a record of visual experiences
that we want to remember. Photographs can also show
details of movement the eye could never catch.

Identifying the subject

The first creative step in taking a photograph is to choose the subject. This may seem obvious, but any one situation usually offers a wide range of choices. As a general rule, you should look for a subject that will make a single strong point. The more elements there are in the scene, the more important it is to have a clear idea about what you want the picture to show at the moment you press the shutter. If there are too many details in the viewfinder that do not support the main point, the picture will tend to look untidy – a random snap rather than an effective photograph. As we have just seen, the camera, unlike the eye, is not capable of concentrating on what is interesting and ignoring the rest. Everything in the viewfinder tends to have equal prominence

unless the photographer organizes the scene and selects the image to bring out a particular part or aspect of it.

With an inherently disorganized scene – a crowded beach, for example – you need a good deal of skill to produce a broad view that does not look untidy, although the rich variety seen in a panoramic shot may have its own interest. The solution may be to find a viewpoint that allows you to simplify the picture down to a few elements. The photographs on these two pages illustrate three ways of simplifying the picture – moving in on a subject, pointing the camera downward to cut out extraneous background detail, and using a vertical format to concentrate on a single figure.

A conventional panorama of the beach records the overall scene without directing your attention to any feature in particular. The subject is full of other interesting photographic possibilities.

The solitary bather (right) is the subject rather than the confusion of surf. Attention is drawn to her by the footprints the photographer has carefully lined up in the viewfinder before taking the picture.

A downward shot from a hotel balcony produces a forceful picture because the photographer chose as a subject the strong graphic pattern of umbrellas and sunbathers.

A close–up of a little girl's delight as a wave leaves her stranded excludes distracting detail and frames her as the entire subject of the picture within a plain blue background.

Studied images, fleeting moments

Sometimes the world around us moves so fast that we experience moments of action, excitement or laughter almost as a passing blur. The camera's ability to freeze these moments and record them on film is one of photography's most remarkable attributes and many of the pictures that give greatest pleasure are those that exploit it. But in other photographs what impresses is the sense of absolute stillness and order. This is often the result of the photographer's having had time to think hard about a stationary scene and perhaps rearrange it to make an image that is thoroughly balanced, as in the picture of a hotel balcony on this page.

There are thus two contrasting approaches to taking pictures. On the one hand, an alert photographer can capture those high points and instants in time that may never return – a child's first faltering steps, or a spontaneous burst of laughter in a game. The only way to be sure of catching these fleeting events consistently is to learn to anticipate them. This means having the camera ready, out of its case, with the film wound on and the controls set to the approximate light conditions and focusing distance. From then on, it is a matter of quick reactions, accurate timing – and a little luck – to be able to capture pictures with the immediacy of the two images at the top of the page opposite.

The other, more considered, approach requires patience together with something of the artist's eye for composition. With time and care, even the simplest objects can be arranged to make an attractive picture and one that perhaps is alive in a different way – because it is charged with atmosphere. The key to successful pictures of this kind is often the lighting, which may be precisely controlled by the photographer. Even natural light can be controlled, if only by standing at a well-judged angle to the subject you are photographing or by waiting for the transformations in a landscape that occur as the sun moves or is covered by clouds.

The warmth and peace of a holiday balcony is evoked precisely in an image that seems as casual as the towel draped on the chair. In fact the photographer carefully studied the angle of the chair, adjusted the louvred doors as a frame, and waited until the sun lit the green slats on one side, leaving the others dark.

Landscapes like the one at right may last only seconds as sunlight bursts through storm clouds. The photographer had foreseen the dramatic instant of brilliant contrast.

A gust of wind flips off the cyclist's hat –
but the photographer was ready to catch
the instant of surprise and amusement. He
had preset the camera controls as the
cyclist approached a corner.

Spontaneity and contrivance mix in this
picture by a photographer who gave the
boy the bubble gum so that he would relax
for the camera – and then snapped off a
remarkably natural and relaxed portrait.

A moment's thought

Many first-time camera users set about taking pictures assuming that everything will fall automatically into place. They aim the lens directly towards the subject, lining up the most important features with the centre of the viewfinder as though the camera were a kind of rifle and the subject a target. This approach will certainly record the subject on film, but is unlikely to produce an appealing image. You will achieve better results by thinking for a few seconds and allowing yourself time to study the scene in the viewfinder carefully. Are there distracting elements in the frame that would be better excluded by changing the camera position? Is a vertical format – used for the shot here of the reflected building – more suited to the subject than a horizontal one? Are there patterns – as in the rodeo picture – that can be used to give the picture a bold visual structure? With practice, this self-questioning process becomes automatic, a rapid sequence of mental trial and error. But for the beginner – and even for the expert – a conscious pause for thought can make all the difference between an ordinary snapshot and a picture with real impact.

A few simple ideas can point the way. First, placing the main subject slightly off-centre in the frame can create a more balanced and visually satisfying effect than composing directly around the picture's centre. The picture of the old woman opposite is a fine example. Pay particular attention to any lines in the scene – they can be used to direct the attention of a viewer around the picture. Strong lines can also affect the mood you want to achieve – diagonals suggest direction and even movement, and are useful for leading the eye into and out of the picture. These are only a few of the elements of composition that you should take into account in making a picture something more than a visual jumble – and many more will become apparent as you begin to develop visual awareness.

Closing in on this row of cowgirls and using a vertical format eliminates the confused background of a rodeo scene – a simple yet often effective compositional technique. The real subject is the central woman, framed by her two similarly dressed companions. Though they are abruptly cropped by the picture's edge, they are still important in providing pattern and balancing the whole image.

Alone in a wheatfield, the child dominates the landscape although occupying only a small part of the picture area. The photographer moved back and up the hill to keep horizon and sky out of the shot and make the wheatfield into a single, simple background of warm colour.

Reflections can produce intriguing images. Here, amateur Herb Gustafson used observation and forethought to frame the clock tower of the old Federal Courthouse at St Paul, Minnesota, as a reflected vertical in the glass wall of a modern building opposite.

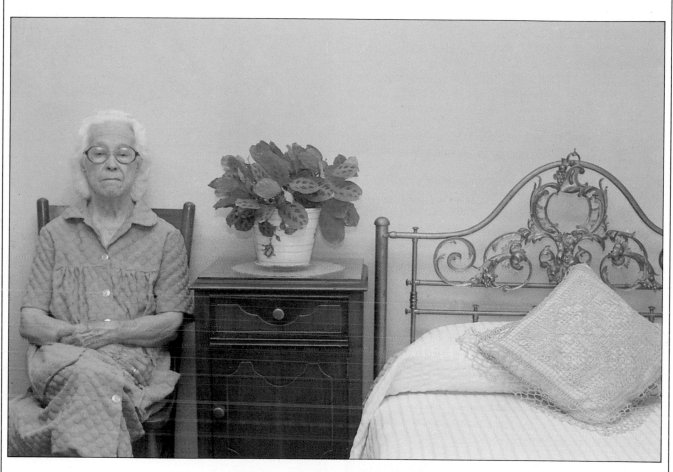

A remarkable portrait of old age, *full of atmosphere,*
relies for its impact on an imaginative composition in which the
subject appears at the very edge of the frame. Centre stage is
occupied by an unassuming potted plant. The visual balance
between the old woman and the bed, with its quilt similar in colour
to her clothing, helps convey the sense of silence and stillness.

Individual vision

Every good photographer eventually develops a way of taking pictures that is personal and distinctive. A few are lucky enough to have such an individual way of seeing that this distinctiveness surfaces from the moment they pick up a camera. To others it comes later, as they gradually begin to master the mechanics of taking pictures.

Experimentation is important, because if you try different approaches you are more likely to discover the type of picture-taking that suits you best. As a starting point, concentrate your interest on a particular subject – you may be drawn to photographing a close companion, or landscapes, or sports, or close-up details. This does not mean you have to stick exclusively to a favourite subject to develop a style. Zeroing in on one target eliminates the uncertainties of less familiar subjects or situations so you can centre your efforts on experimentation and perhaps identify an approach that is essentially your own. You may discover that you are at heart a romantic, finding interest and scope in dreamy images such as the picture of the girl here, or that you are less interested in the superficial descriptive side of a subject than in such purely visual qualities as the rich colours and strong abstract pattern of the fence shown below.

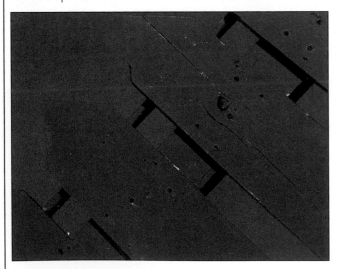

The bold stark pattern of a red fence tilted to march across the sky shows an approach that is the complete opposite of the main picture. Yet for all its impersonality, this image, too, conveys a strong personal style. For this photographer, clean lines, pure colours, and abstract patterns are the essential pictorial elements.

The delicacy of this child's features is effectively enhanced by the gauzy quality of the photograph. Her face is framed by the diffused green, sympathetic in tone to her light eyes. The thoughtful gesture of the hand adds a pleasing pensive mood, unexpected in one so young.

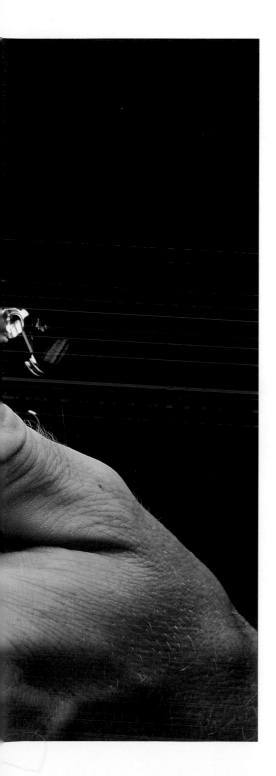

YOU AND YOUR CAMERA

Photography combines two different areas of skill. On the one hand, you need to develop an ability to see creatively, identifying interesting and appealing visual aspects of the world around you. But you also need the ability to translate these photographic ideas into pictures. The camera and film can become efficient servants of your creative impulse – if you learn how to use them.

This is partly a question of mastering essential photographic skills – the principles of camera handling, focusing and exposure that apply to all cameras, however complex or simple. You will handle a camera more confidently if you have a clear understanding of the basic relationship between light, camera and film as explained in the following pages. Try to develop a close familiarity with your own camera also, so that using its controls becomes second nature. The functions and operation of these controls are explained here, but you must study your own camera to see how the principles can be most effectively applied.

Finally, consider your camera in relation to the type of photographs you intend to take. Know the limitations of your equipment and work within them. You will need a camera with a fast shutter to freeze rapid movement, for example. But if you already have one why not go and find some exciting action so as to test the camera's fastest speed? Photography is most enjoyable when you have equipment that extends slightly beyond your current capabilities or needs. As your skill grows, you will value the greater versatility your camera provides.

Good technique is here symbolized by a graphic image that suggests the photographer's sure-handed mastery of the camera's controls in framing and sharply focusing his subject.

Light, lens and film

The word photography means "drawing with light," a phrase that conveys both the creative and the chemical nature of the photographic process. A camera is simply a device for bringing together in a sharp image the light reflected from a scene and allowing it briefly to touch a film material so sensitive that the light leaves a trace, which can be developed into a finished picture.

To form an image, light has only to pass through a pinhole into a dark area and fall on a screen. The modern camera uses a lens and variable-size opening, or aperture, instead of a simple hole, and has a shutter that allows light in for fractions of time, which the photographer can control.

The advantage of a lens is that it can gather and focus light into a sharp, bright image. After collecting the light rays scattering out from every point on the subject, the lens bends them through precisely determined angles to meet again as points. These countless points, varying in colour and brightness; form an image that is an exact copy of the subject's pattern of light. As shown in the diagram, the rays of light travel through the lens in such a way that this image arrives upside down and reversed, with light from the top of the subject brought to focus at the bottom of the image.

The film lies behind the lens on the plane where the light rays form a sharp image when the lens is focused for distant subjects. As a subject gets closer to the camera, its sharp image falls farther and farther behind the lens; hence, the lens must be moved forward in order to keep the image in focus on the film.

When the photographer opens the shutter, light from the subject begins to act on an emulsion coating on the film that contains crystals of silver halides. These salts of silver are extremely light-sensitive. They darken when exposed to light, much as skin tans in sunlight – but infinitely quicker. The light triggers a chemical change in the salts so that they start to form microscopic grains of black silver. Where more light strikes the film, more crystals are triggered. This process, however, is not visible to the naked eye, and the film requires chemical development before an image of the black silver pattern appears. The lightest areas of the subject – such as the sky – look black because they caused most silver to form, while shadow areas that sent no light to the film appear blank. The result is a *negative* image, which can be reversed in printing to make a *positive* image – re-creating the tones (and with colour films, the colours) of the original scene.

Anatomy of a camera

The parts of a camera, reduced to a schematic form, show in essence what a simple apparatus it is – a box for gathering and forming an image of the subject. Cameras come in many different shapes and sizes, but they all operate on the basic principles shown below.

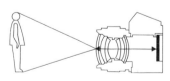

The lens brings the image into sharp focus on the film. Moving the lens forward or back changes the lens-to-film distance, focusing near or far subjects.

The aperture regulates the light entering the camera, usually by means of an iris diaphragm. This is a continuously variable ring of overlapping metal blades.

The shutter controls the length of time light falls onto the film. A common type exposes the film through an opening between two blinds that travel across the film.

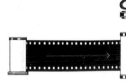

The film, held flat at the focal plane, receives the image and records it. The film is wound on after each exposure, permitting a number of shots on each roll.

The camera you use/1

The variety of camera shapes and sizes may seem bewildering, but there is good reason for this diversity: cameras are designed for different tasks as well as different price brackets. Some are ideal for snapshots, and other, bigger cameras are more suited to applications that demand an image of very high quality.

Of all the different types, the 35mm camera is the most convenient compromise between image quality and ease of use. The term "35mm" refers to the width of the film, which comes in a long sprock-etted strip, loaded into a metal cassette. The actual size of a standard 35mm negative is $1 \times 1\frac{1}{2}$ inches – large enough to make quality prints as big as this page, but small enough for the camera that carries it to be reasonably compact.

The term for the most popular type of 35mm camera – single lens reflex, or SLR for short – refers to its viewing system, which makes the camera extremely easy to use. A mirror reflects light from the single lens up to the viewfinder and shows exactly what is going to appear on film. Focusing and composing the picture is thus made simple. In addition, the SLR is highly versatile because its lens is removable and can be replaced by others that give different views or perform specialized tasks.

Although now the most popular type, the SLR is not the only 35mm camera. "Compact" cameras, for example, usually have a non-interchangeable lens, and their functions, including focusing, may be fully automatic. These cameras are even easier to use than an SLR, but are not as versatile.

Similar to the compact is the rangefinder camera, such as the famous Leica. Small and very quiet in operation, these are best in situations where the photographer wishes to go unnoticed. But range-finders – particularly those with interchangeable lenses – are also useful for general photography when rapid focusing is needed.

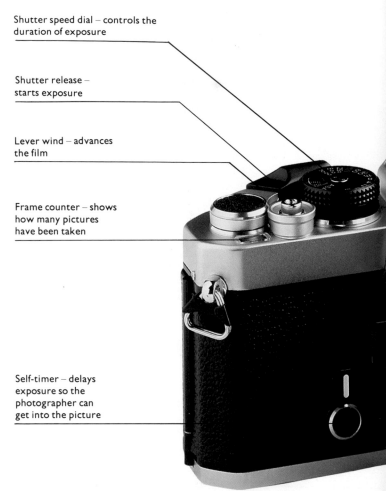

Shutter speed dial – controls the duration of exposure

Shutter release – starts exposure

Lever wind – advances the film

Frame counter – shows how many pictures have been taken

Self-timer – delays exposure so the photographer can get into the picture

35mm SLR
The distinctive shape of the 35mm SLR is due to its viewing system. The camera is instantly recognizable by the central hump, housing the viewing prism and eyepiece. Modern SLRs are smaller than their predecessors, but they must still incorporate a reflex mirror behind the lens, so they are generally bigger and heavier than non-reflex 35mm cameras such as compacts and rangefinders. SLRs range from simple, manually operated types to highly sophisticated electronically controlled models. Even the simplest, however, incorporates a light-measuring system to advise on exposure. And they can all be used under a wide range of conditions.

SLR viewing system
The mirror and pentaprism in an SLR camera (left) let you see the image formed by the lens exactly as it will fall on the film. Light passing through the lens is reflected by the mirror onto a focusing screen, positioned at the same distance from the lens as is the film. This image is then converted by a five-sided prism (the pentaprism) so it can be viewed right way up and right way round. The mirror flips up out of the way when the shutter is released, thus allowing the light to reach the film.

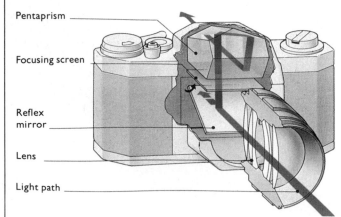

Pentaprism

Focusing screen

Reflex mirror

Lens

Light path

Accessory shoe –
holds a flash unit

Rewind knob – winds
the film back into the
cassette after exposure

Auxiliary flash contact –
connects a remote flash unit
not attached via the
accessory shoe

Aperture ring –
adjusts the iris
diaphragm

Focusing ring –
brings near and
far subjects into
sharp focus

Rangefinder window – forms a
secondary image of out-of-focus
subjects in the viewfinder

Focusing lever –
adjusts focus

Rangefinder camera

These cameras take their name from the quick and easy
method of focusing that they employ – they have an optical
rangefinder that shows in the viewfinder a double image of
out-of-focus subjects. As the lens is focused, the two
images unite to form one. Exposure control is generally
manual or partly automatic. The model shown here has
through-the-lens metering and an interchangeable
lens; it is light and compact but versatile.

Twin autofocus windows –
admit light to the focusing
mechanism

Built-in flash –
supplies extra
light if needed

35mm film

The metal cassette in which
35mm film is supplied is
almost lighttight, but
should still be loaded into
the camera out of the sun.
The processed film produces
prints, or slides in 2 × 2 inch
mounts to fit a projector.

Compact 35mm camera

These simple, lightweight cameras take the same film as SLRs
but often have an easy loading system. Exposure controls
vary from model to model, but most are automatic. Built-in
flash, which pops up for use, is common. Most compacts
have a moderate wide-angle lens, which gives a wider field
of view and greater depth of field. The compact camera
above is typical of the newest models, with automatic
exposure, focusing, flash and film advance.

The camera you use/2

Because photographers have such varied requirements, cameras have evolved in a number of different directions. Although the 35mm SLR can cope with most situations, some people find it too heavy and bulky. Others want a camera that will enable them to see their pictures immediately. And still others, particularly professionals, want the greater technical precision that larger-format cameras can provide.

Pocket cameras, such as the disc and 110 film types shown here, get around the problem of size and weight by using a negative only a fraction the size of the 35mm format. These cameras employ snug-fitting drop-in film cartridges and are so small that they can be carried conveniently at all times. In spite of the inevitable limitations of film size, and general versatility, some 35mm photographers find them useful for snapshots: picture-taking is almost fool-proof and prints are usually of adequate quality up to postcard size.

Instant-picture cameras, though cumbersome by comparison, have different advantages. They eliminate the wait while films are being printed. Immediately after you press the shutter, the camera ejects the print. The picture begins to appear within a few seconds and is fully developed in a matter of minutes. These cameras are fun to use at parties and family occasions because everyone can see the results immediately, and if a picture is a failure there is still a chance to take another. Local laboratories can make extra copies of the same image. Professionals wanting a precisely controlled result often use instant-picture film to judge the effectiveness of a scene or a lighting set-up before taking the shot with conventional film.

When the finest quality is more important than ease of operation, some photographers prefer to use a larger film size than 35mm, even though this means a correspondingly larger camera. The most common of these larger films is 120 rollfilm, which produces negatives $2\frac{1}{4}$ inches (6 cm) wide. Cameras that use this film are bulkier, heavier and mostly costlier than smaller formats, and are usually manually operated rather than being automated. Advanced photographers prefer them, though, because they are not too large to be hand-held and yet they produce a negative of fine quality, capable of showing sharp detail even when the prints need to be blown up into pictures many times the size of the original negatives.

For near-perfect results, some photographers use large-format technical cameras. These take film supplied in individual sheets, usually no smaller than four by five inches in size. As a result, the cameras are somewhat unwieldy and require real expertise.

Pocket and disc cameras

The small 110 and disc models shown here are sophisticated, with automatic exposure, built-in flash and sometimes a switch to change the lens from wide to narrow angle of view, or from long-shots to close-ups. All of them are easy to load, and some have a folding cover to protect the lens when the camera is not in use.

Both disc and 110 cameras are used mainly with colour print film, enlarged to postcard-sized prints. Bigger enlargements look acceptable if the picture is sharp.

Instant-picture cameras

All instant cameras have automatic exposure and a manual control to lighten or darken the results. Some focus automatically, and may have a built-in flash and a capacity for close-ups. The types shown fold flat for easy carrying. For good results, always hold an instant camera steady as the print ejects, and keep your fingers clear of the exit slot.

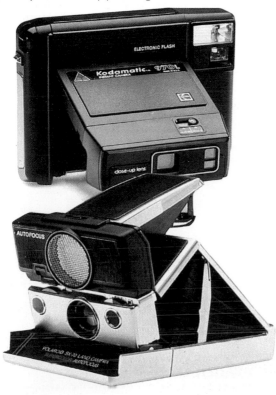

Rollfilm cameras

The most popular medium-format camera is the 120 rollfilm SLR, which, like the 35mm SLR, uses a mirror to reflect the image up to a focusing screen. Rollfilm SLRs often have special film magazines that allow film to be changed from colour to black-and-white or instant film in mid-roll. Their large film size gives exceptional quality.

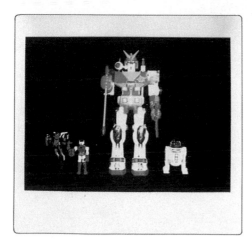

Instant film comes in closed packs that are placed in the camera. The ejected prints are sealed in plastic. The image appears as you watch, colours gradually growing stronger.

Rollfilm gives images $2\frac{1}{4}$ inches (6 cm) wide, but of different heights, depending on the camera type. A square format $2\frac{1}{4} \times 2\frac{1}{4}$ inches (6 cm × 6 cm), as shown here, is the commonest.

What to do first

Nothing is more disappointing than taking a whole series of pictures and then discovering that the film did not wind through because of incorrect loading in the first place. Step one in photography is to load the camera correctly. Then, using the procedures on the opposite page, set the correct film speed – the sensitivity of the film you have put in – and check to make sure that the camera's exposure meter is working properly.

You can load disc and 110 cameras quickly and safely, even in bright sunlight, just by dropping in a new cartridge and winding on to the first frame. But cassettes of 35mm film are not entirely lightproof, so cameras using this film should be loaded and unloaded in the shade or indoors. And although

some cameras now take up 35mm film automatically, a leading strip or tongue of film usually has to be carefully threaded onto the camera's take-up spool. After closing the back, there are a couple of ways to check that the film has not slipped out of the spool and that the film is actually advancing when you wind the lever. The simplest way is to turn the rewind knob gently in a clockwise direction. After taking up slack, the film should begin to pull taut, transmitting resistance to the knob. (This is also the best way to check whether you have film in a camera.) You can make doubly sure the film is advancing properly by checking that the rewind knob turns when you wind ahead. Eventually, these simple checks become almost automatic.

Rewind knob – returns film to cassette. Also used to open camera back

Sprockets – advance film frame by frame

Film chamber – holds the film cassette

Take-up spool – accepts tongue of film in slot

Loading a 35mm camera

I–In the shade, hold the camera firmly by the lens and pull up the rewind knob to open the camera back. Keep the knob raised.

2–Place the film in the left-hand chamber, then push in the rewind knob, turning it until it clicks firmly down into place.

3–Turn the film lip forward and insert the tongue into one of the slits in the take-up spool. Fit the bottom row of holes over the sprockets.

4–Next, click the shutter and wind on to ensure that the sprockets begin to engage both top and bottom rows of perforations.

Checking the meter

Usually you switch the meter on by cocking the shutter (right), by lightly pressing the shutter release, or by using a meter switch. If the meter is working properly, a meter display will be activated, as in the example shown at far right. With more simple models that use a needle indicator, make sure that the needle moves when the camera is pointed at a bright subject. Many cameras

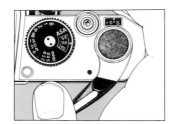

have special devices for checking the battery power. On some, a battery check button can be pressed. Sometimes a warning light shows automatically when power is reduced.

Film perforations – catch on sprockets

Film speed – indicates sensitivity of the film to light

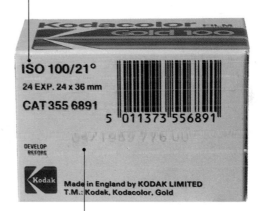

Film expiration date – shows date by which film should be used for best results

5–Close the camera back and continue advancing the film until the number for the first exposure appears in the exposure counter window.

6–To unload, release the rewind catch or button, lift the rewind crank, and turn it clockwise until it suddenly turns more easily.

Setting film speed

The film speed is marked on the film box and on the cassette or cartridge. Some 110 cameras set the speed automatically when the cartridge is inserted. But 35mm cameras have a film speed dial that must be set manually to match the speed of the film loaded. When shooting, check occasionally in case the dial has been moved accidentally.

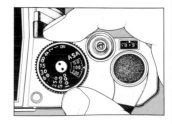

Keeping steady

For sharp, well-framed pictures, you must hold the camera absolutely still while you release the shutter. Camera shake at the moment of exposure is by far the most common cause of blurred or crooked pictures. The sequence of actions involved in bringing the camera to the eye, adjusting the controls and pressing the shutter in a smooth, stable way needs to be rehearsed until it becomes automatic. Experienced photographers are said to think through their hands because they are so familiar with their cameras that they handle them almost by second nature.

To achieve a firm but comfortable camera hold for both horizontal and vertical pictures, you can vary the exact grip to suit your own hands and camera. But you should make sure to cradle the camera securely, with the controls within easy reach of your fingers. While aiming, rest your index finger lightly on the shutter release so you can press it gently and smoothly at the decisive moment. Holding your breath as you release the shutter may help to minimize movement.

Wherever possible, take advantage of any additional support, as shown below. Extra stability becomes crucial when you are making slower exposures – in evening light or dim interiors, for example. Take special care with 110 cameras, because their light weight and flat shape may increase the risk of shake, which can show up in prints enlarged from the small negative.

Holding a 110 camera
Some 110s have steadying handles to minimize camera shake. Hold others firmly at each end and remember to keep your fingers clear of the lens. For vertical pictures with built-in flash, keep the flash uppermost.

Holding a 35mm SLR
For both horizontal and vertical shots, grip the camera with your right hand, using the index finger to release the shutter and the thumb to wind on. Use your left hand to support camera and lens, and to adjust focus.

Steadying the shot
Using a standard lens at shutter speeds of 1/125 or faster, working without support is safe enough. Stand squarely, feet apart, with the elbows tucked well into the body. At 1/60, look for some means of steadying yourself: lean against a wall or, for lower viewpoints, try sitting cross-legged with your elbows on your knees – or lying down with your weight on your elbows. At even slower speeds in dim lighting conditions the camera requires additional rigid support. Rest it on a flat surface or hold it against a wall if you do not have a tripod.

Steady, level and carefully composed, this shot of the Statue of Liberty seen against the World Trade Center shows the result of good camera handling. The strong lines of the buildings are carefully aligned with the picture frame.

Camera shake

When you are taking pictures in dim light, you will usually need slow shutter speeds to let enough light into the camera. The results may be entirely blurred, as above, unless some support is found for the camera.

Crooked pictures

It is very important to hold the camera straight, especially if your subject has strong horizontal or vertical lines. A sloping horizon or apparently leaning buildings can ruin a picture (above). Make sure that the true verticals, particularly in buildings, are aligned with an edge of the viewfinder frame.

Focusing the image

To achieve sharp images you need not only to hold the camera steady but also to focus it accurately. The camera cannot keep near and far objects flexibly in focus, as the eye does, and the blurring of out-of-focus objects is one of photography's most distinctive characteristics.

In most pictures, the zone that looks reasonably sharp extends for some distance behind and in front of the plane on which you focus the lens. The depth of this zone depends on several factors, including the size of the lens aperture, as pages 44-45 explain. But the diagram on the right, here, shows that one of the most important factors is the distance of the subject from the lens. The closer you are to the subject of your picture, the more carefully you must select the part you want to be most sharp and clear.

To adjust the position of sharpest focus, all cameras except the most simple have a focusing control ring. This moves the lens forward and backward to change the lens's distance from the film. Moving the lens and film farther apart brings into focus objects closer to the camera.

With some cameras, you focus by estimating your distance from the main subject and matching this to a scale of distance markings or symbols around the lens. Because this method of focusing involves guesswork, however, other, more versatile, cameras have systems that indicate clearly in the viewfinder when the image is sharp. The SLR camera uses a precision mirror to reflect onto a screen the image that will appear on the film, allowing you to adjust the lens until the screened image is sharp.

Most SLR focusing screens nowadays are made of finely moulded plastic. At the centre are focusing aids – often a pair of semicircular prisms that split any unsharp image across the middle. As you turn the lens to bring the image gradually into focus, the two broken halves move together to form a perfectly aligned picture.

These twin prisms are together called a split-image finder, and around them – or sometimes instead of them – is a ring of tiny prisms of a similar type. These microprisms have the same effect of breaking up the image, but on a smaller scale, so that the unsharp picture appears shattered into countless shimmering fragments.

Rangefinder cameras have separate lenses for viewing the subject and exposing the film, so they rely on a less direct method of focusing. When you look into the viewfinder, you see a double image of the subject, and you turn the focusing ring until these images move together and coincide. In most autofocus cameras, an electronic eye performs the task of judging when the two images meet, and the lens is automatically adjusted for correct focus.

The focusing control ring
Turning the wide, knurled ring focuses subjects at varying distances (indicated in feet and metres just under the ring). The ring moves the lens farther from the film for a subject only 3 ft away (left) than for far subjects (right), which are indicated by a symbol representing infinity (∞).

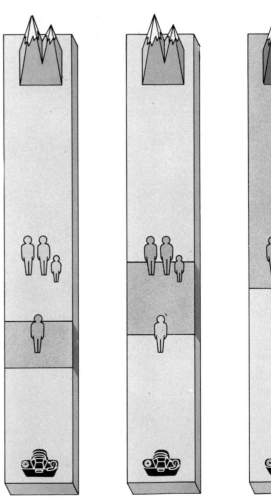

How much is in focus?
At close distances, only a very shallow part of a scene appears sharp (red zone above left). If you are taking a head-and-shoulders portrait, for example, at a range of a few feet, the background will blur (ochre area). The zone of sharp focus becomes progressively wider as you focus on more distant subjects (central group) until eventually the lens brings into focus objects in a zone stretching far back from the middle distance.

SLR focusing
The split-image finder focusing screen – which appears as a bull's-eye in the unfocused image at right – makes SLR focusing easy. Look for a horizontal or vertical edge near the centre of the subject (here the window frame) and turn the focusing ring until the two split halves in the circle coincide (below). Alternatively, focus until the microprism clears.

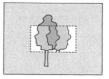

Rangefinder focusing
The typical rangefinder system shows a double image in the viewfinder when the subject is out of focus (above left). The difference between this and the single image of a correctly focused subject is clear enough for focusing to be rapid and sure even in dim light – when focusing an SLR sometimes becomes difficult.

Autofocusing
The compact autofocusing camera here has a tiny motor that moves the lens to focus on the area indicated by a distance measuring system. This system compares two differing views of the nearest object in the centre of the camera's viewfinder – doing this so quickly that it seems to be virtually instantaneous. Other systems bounce sound or infra-red rays off subjects. Some SLRs have a support autofocus system with viewfinder lights (bottom right) acting as focus guides.

The shutter

The shutter is the basic picture-taking control on a camera. Releasing it smoothly, at just the right moment, makes all the difference to a shot. Never hurry – the secret of sharp, well-timed pictures is to be ready, and anticipate the moment, squeezing the release gently when you feel everything in the viewfinder is perfect.

Choosing the right shutter speed is just as important. It affects both sharpness and exposure. The numbers on the shutter speed dial are called speeds but they are actually exposure times – fractions of a second for which the shutter will stay open, exposing the film to the light image projected by the lens. For simplicity, 30 is used to mean 1/30 second, and 60 to mean 1/60 second. The higher the number, the faster the speed and the briefer the exposure. At each higher setting, exposure time is halved. Most single lens reflex cameras have a fastest speed of 1/1000 second, but SLRs with a top speed of 1/2000 second and even 1/4000 second are also available.

For a sharp picture, the fastest practical shutter speed is the safest to use, because the less time during which light from an image falls onto the film, the less time there is for any subject movement or camera shake to blur the photograph. Camera shake while the shutter is open is probably the commonest cause of disappointing pictures.

A safe working speed for handheld shots with a normal lens is 1/125 second – fast enough to stop camera shake and freeze all except rapid motion. Close-ups and shots with telephoto lenses need faster speeds – 1/250 or 1/500 second – and so do active scenes such as children playing.

In practice, the choice is often limited by the lighting – in dimmer light longer exposures are needed, and this makes it difficult to freeze movement. On dull days or indoors, speeds below 1/60 second may be required for an adequate picture, and then it is necessary to provide the camera with a support – if possible, use a tripod and a cable release.

At slow shutter speeds, any movement blurs the image. *In the picture below of a girl roller skating in a park, a speed of 1/30 dissolves her whole body into streaks of colour.*

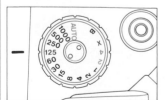

Shutter speed control
Shutter speed is usually set by means of a dial on top of the camera (above). Other systems include a ring positioned around the lens mount.

The shutter scale
The range of shutter speeds offered by your camera will include most of the speeds on the scale at right. The more versatile the camera, the more speeds will be offered. The dial at left, for example, runs from 4 secs to 1/1000. Other settings offered are "B" for longer exposures, "X" for flash synchronization and "Auto" (sometimes "A") for automatic exposure.

Slow speeds				
4 secs	2 secs	1 sec	1/2	1/4

Camera handling

Slow speeds are suitable not only for static subjects but also when you want to suggest movement impressionistically. The lights of city traffic at night (left) have been blurred into vivid, rushing streaks by using a shutter speed of 1/4.

At medium speeds (*here 1/125*)*, there is still some blur, but it shows mainly in the hands and feet – the parts of the body that are moving at greatest speed.*

Fast shutter speeds *will freeze all movement. At 1/500, the girl's body, hands and feet are sharp, even though she is racing toward the camera at full tilt.*

		Medium speeds		Fast speeds			
1/8	1/15	1/30	1/60	1/125	1/250	1/500	1/1000	1/2000

Camera support needed — Extra care required with handheld camera — Safe to handhold with normal lenses — Safe to handhold with telephoto lenses →

Medium speeds are the usual choice for everyday scenes, and are also needed for flash pictures, such as the one at left. Many cameras have a speed marked X (usually 1/60 or 1/90). When you set the dial to this, the flash and shutter are synchronized.

Fast speeds of above 1/500 are useful for action pictures or with high-powered lenses, which magnify movement and are difficult to hold steady. The flashing hooves of the racehorses on the left were frozen with a shutter speed of 1/1000.

The aperture

The aperture is the opening of the lens through which light enters the camera. On all but the simplest cameras, you can increase or decrease the opening, usually by means of an iris diaphragm, and this is one of the principal ways of controlling how the picture will look. Widening the aperture allows more light to reach the film. Together with shutter speed (which controls the amount of time during which light can affect the film), this determines the exposure – the total amount of light that reaches the film. The other important function of the aperture is that it affects depth of field – the zone of sharp focus in a scene, extending from the nearest element that is sharp to the farthest. Because wrong focus is less noticeable if the effective lens area is reduced, depth of field increases as aperture size decreases.

Aperture is adjusted in a series of click stops, each full stop doubling or halving the amount of light let in. These stops are marked on the aperture control ring in a coded numerical series called f-numbers, running in a standard sequence f/1, f/1.4, f/2, f/2.8, f/4, f/5.6, f/8, f/11, f/16, f/22. The numbers get bigger as the aperture opening gets smaller. F/16 is thus a small aperture, letting in much less light than f/2. No matter what size or type of lens you have, the system ensures that the same f-number will let the same amount of light reach the film.

The lowest f-number shown on the aperture control ring indicates the largest aperture a particular lens can provide, often between f/1.4 and f/2. To let you view the subject clearly, modern lenses usually stay open at maximum aperture until you press the shutter, then the aperture "stops down" to the selected f-number. This means that you have enough light to focus the main subject sharply while you are viewing – but that near and far objects may look fuzzy, because the aperture has not yet stopped down and improved the depth of field. Most cameras now have a preview button (below). When pressed. it alters the image in the viewfinder to show the actual extent of sharpness.

SLR preview button
This is often on, or by, the lens. You simply press it to preview the true depth of field of the aperture.

Aperture scale
The sequence of f-stops is shown at right, light being halved at each setting. The pictures below the scale show the effect on exposure if the aperture is reduced without slowing the shutter speed. By using a preview button, you can see the image darkening at each stop as the aperture steadily cuts the light admitted.

At maximum aperture, used for the picture below, depth of field is very shallow. Only the main focused subject is sharp. Foreground and background are blurred.

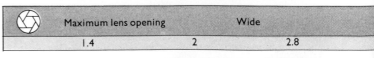

	Maximum lens opening	Wide	
1.4	2	2.8

f/2 Bright image, shallow depth of field

f/2.8 One stop down

At a medium aperture, depth of field is greater. The farthest child and most of the background are sharp. But the boy in the foreground is still out of focus.

At minimum aperture, depth of field is so great that even the foreground boy is sharp. The shot needed a slow shutter speed at this aperture, so any movement would have blurred.

		Medium		Small		Minimum lens opening
4	5.6	8	11	16	22	

f/4 Two stops down

f/5.6 Three stops down

f/8 Four stops down

f/11 Five stops down, good depth of field

The right film

In selecting what kind of film to put in the camera, the broad choice lies between film for colour prints, for colour slides or for pictures in black-and-white (overleaf). Within these categories are many different types of film – it is easier to take successful shots if the film chosen matches the subject and lighting conditions as precisely as possible.

The most important property of a film is its sensitivity to light – the film speed. Slow films need much more light to form a usable image than do fast films, which are highly sensitive. This means that you can more easily take pictures in dim light with fast film. In brighter light, fast film allows you to select a fast shutter speed or a small aperture if needed. However, fast films have one drawback: the grains that make up the image have to be large so that they react quickly to a limited amount of light, and when the picture is blown up they show as gritty texture. Slow films have smaller grains and can record finer detail, but unless the light is bright, they may force the photographer to use an unsuitably slow shutter speed or too wide an aperture. In average daylight, films of medium or medium-fast speed offer a good compromise. Fast films are an advantage in poor light or for action photographs requiring fast shutter speeds. Slow films are useful for static, detailed subjects, such as still-life or architecture.

Until recently, film speed has been indicated by an ASA (American Standards Association) number, or by a DIN (Deutsche Industrie Norm) number, and the ASA number appears first in the new ISO (International Standards Organization) system of designating speed. Thus, a marking ISO 100/21° (or simply ISO 100) indicates ASA 100 or 21°DIN – a medium speed. Each doubling or halving of the ISO number indicates a halving or doubling of speed, changing the exposure required by one full setting on either the aperture or shutter speed scales.

For fine detail, as in this shot of a tub of chillies in a market stall, slow film is best. the Kodachrome 25 film for slides used here has extremely fine grain (seen in the inset microscopic enlargement), and many professionals like it.

In average light, medium-speed film works well, needing not too wide an aperture and showing little grain (inset). This picture of the interior of a partly inflated hot-air balloon was shot on Ektachrome 64 film for slides.

Film speed
The film speed rating and other details are clearly marked on the box, as at left. Kodacolor VR400 film – a fast film for colour prints – takes its name from the ISO speed rating, which is numerically the same as the old ASA rating. You set the camera to the film speed by lining up the corresponding number on the rewind knob or the shutter speed dial (bottom left). The guide to film speeds (right) shows the range and differing sensitivities.

	ISO	Slow			
Color prints					
Color slides		25		50	64
Black-and-white		25	32	50	

Slow film (ISO 25) can be bought only in black-and-white or colour slide form. Choose it whenever fine detail is important, provided you have strong light or can give a long exposure.

Medium-speed films (ISO 50 to 100) offer fine-quality results but can still be used in below-average lighting conditions. They are available in colour and in black-and-white.

Dim light or fast action calls for fast film. There was just enough light on this modern building at dusk for a hand-held picture on Ektachrome 400 film. In big enlargements, however, grain is noticeable, as the inset shows.

					Fast
100		200	400	1000	
100		200	400		
100	125		400		1250

High-speed films (up to ISO 200) are useful when the light is changeable and for many action subjects.

Very-high-speed film (ISO 400) is useful in a wide range of situations, from poor light to rapid action. The results are usually good, and this film is now very popular.

Extremely-high-speed films (above ISO 400) are useful only when light is too low for any other type. They tend to be grainy and are used relatively seldom.

Choosing black-and-white film

Why should anyone use black-and-white film? After all, it is now only slightly cheaper than colour and the bright hues of nature seem a lot to sacrifice. But black-and-white clearly does have a great appeal, and is the chosen medium of many good photographers. What this film lacks in colour, it gains in dramatic impact. Whereas the variety and vibrancy of colour sometimes complicate the appearance of a scene, black-and-white has a graphic simplicity that is well shown in the picture on the opposite page – an ability to convey mood, form and pattern solely in tones of light and dark. You can learn important lessons in photography by using this film, because it is one step farther removed from the real world. Without colour you can more easily concentrate on composing with light, developing a new and valuable way of seeing the world around you.

Black-and-white film has other, more practical advantages. Processing is simple, allowing both development and printing to be carried out at home with relative ease. The equipment needed is neither expensive nor complicated. And home processing allows total control over the final image, including subtle adjustment to the quality of the print.

Black-and-white film is also still available in a wider range of speeds than is colour film. Very slow film (ISO 32 or less) is useful for copying prints onto a new negative or for photography requiring fine detail. Using such film, big enlargements can be made without graininess appearing. At the other end of the scale, ultra-fast film of ISO 1250 will cope with very dim light or fast-moving subjects.

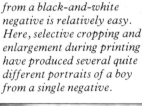

Manipulating prints from a black-and-white negative is relatively easy. Here, selective cropping and enlargement during printing have produced several quite different portraits of a boy from a single negative.

Difficult lighting conditions are much less of a problem in black-and-white than in colour. The superb versatility of monochrome is evident in the evocative portrait of a little girl (left) taken on fast film in low light. The print still contains a full range of delicate tones.

Tone and texture create a powerful abstract image in this high-contrast picture of sand dunes (right). Black-and-white concentrates attention on such qualities.

Prints or slides?

There are two broad categories of colour film – print and slide. Print (or negative) film yields a negative image from which prints are made. Slide (or transparency) film gives positive transparencies. These two types of film are discussed in general here, but their differing characteristics are examined in greater detail on pages 120-123.

Print film is far more popular, mainly because prints are more convenient to look at than slides, and you can display them easily in frames or albums (below). Another advantage is that the printing stage offers an opportunity to correct inaccuracies of exposure. During printing you can also compensate for the unwanted colour effects that result when pictures are taken with daylight colour film in mixed artificial light, and, for example, come out looking unpleasantly orange or green.

Slides, on the other hand, have superior colour quality, with more brilliance, subtlety and depth. They are generally preferred by professionals because they are more suited to reproduction in books or magazines. Even for the amateur, slides can offer greater realism; with a projector, they can be shown greatly enlarged, re-creating scenes on a convincing scale. It is also easier to judge the quality of a slide than that of a negative.

Some photographers take their pictures on slide film, then select the ones they want made into prints, either sending them to a processing laboratory or converting them in a home darkroom. But slide film does demand accuracy in selecting exposure, because you can make only very slight corrections in processing or printing compared to those possible with print film.

False colours will appear when pictures are taken on daylight slide film in artificial light other than flash. However, you can buy films specially balanced to avoid such colour "casts." These special films are compatible both with photographic tungsten lights and with the light from household light bulbs.

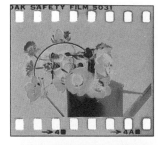

Print quality
To print well, a negative should look sharp like this. Because hues are reversed, evaluating the likely appearance of the finished print can be difficult.

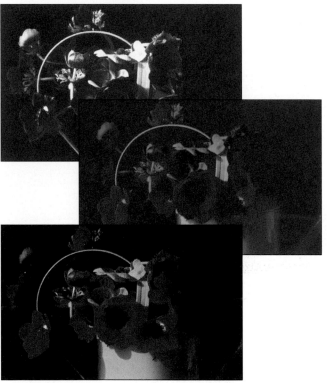

Different results are possible from a negative, as shown above. If you are dissatisfied with the results when your pictures come back, ask for corrected reprints. The top two prints above have unacceptable colour errors.

Colour prints
You can keep prints in a number of different ways. Mounting them in an album not only displays them well but also keeps them clean and flat. You can have special shots enlarged and framed. Remember to store negatives carefully in a dry, cool and dark place – you may want more prints from them later.

Viewing slides

Projectors for slide shows range from simple hand-operated models to magazine-loaded autofocus models as shown at left. If you do not have a screen, a taut sheet, a large piece of white cardboard or even a flat-finish white wall will make do. As an alternative to projecting slides, you can look at them in a simple slide viewer.

GETTING THE EXPOSURE RIGHT

Modern cameras simplify exposure control. Their automatic systems of measuring and regulating the light that enters the camera do most of the work for you. But the camera will not always get it right, because no amount of technological wizardry or computerized circuitry can produce just the picture you want in every situation. Camera systems work to fixed rules, whereas exposing the film often involves a creative choice. In the final analysis, you must yourself decide how you would like the picture to look and, if necessary, overrule the automatic system.

A good camera metering system aims to provide an exposure that is technically correct – one that offers a compromise between the amount of light needed for dark and light areas of the scene. Usually, the result will look fine. Sometimes, however, a particular part of a scene is more important to you than the rest. The camera cannot deduce this, and in settling for an average exposure may over- or underexpose the key area of your composition. This is where your creative choice comes in. Whether you have an automatic or a manually controlled camera, learn to interpret the distribution of light in the scene, and then decide which combination of aperture and shutter will produce the effect you want.

Sun behind the subject makes exposure hard to judge. The camera's meter is bound to read the bright sky and indicate an exposure setting that will cut down the light. In such situations you have to override the meter – as the photographer did here. The amount of light is just right for the three figures, although the meter needle indicates overexposure. With less light, they would have appeared only as silhouettes.

Controlling light

The light reflected from the world around us varies enormously in intensity. On a sunny day, the scene may be several hundred times as bright outdoors as indoors. Our eyes quickly adjust to these different levels of brightness, but film is not as versatile – it needs a precisely fixed amount of light to form a good image. To get correctly exposed pictures you have to control the light that enters the camera, by first measuring the brightness of the scene and then adjusting your aperture and shutter speed until the quantity of light hitting the film exactly matches the film's sensitivity.

Both shutter and aperture halve or double the amount of light reaching the film each time you adjust their control scales by one full step. Thus, controlling the light is a simple matter of increasing or decreasing either the shutter speed or the size of the aperture. If you balance an increase of shutter speed against a decrease of aperture (or vice versa) the total amount of light reaching the film remains constant. As the diagrams below make clear, several different combinations of aperture and shutter speed can give you the same effective exposure.

This is not to say that each combination will produce the same image. In the picture of wine flowing into a glass at bottom left, a fast shutter freezes the movement, but a wide aperture throws the background out of focus. Conversely, as the shutter speed slows and the aperture narrows, the decanter in the background comes into focus but the flowing liquid blurs. Varying the aperture and shutter speed thus gives you creative control over the picture.

In very bright light, there may be a wide range of possible shutter and aperture combinations. But in dim light your choice will be more restricted. The photographer of the mother and child at the foot of the opposite page, for example, could not use too slow a shutter without blurring the picture, and had to choose the widest possible aperture to deliver enough light to the film.

Aperture and shutter speed

These two controls determine exposure in much the same way as length and diameter affect volume: though the disc representing light on the left is short and fat, it has exactly the same volume as the long, thin stick of light on the right – a long exposure at a small aperture.

Think of exposure as an hourglass – just as the same amount of sand runs more quickly through the hourglass on the left, so doubling the aperture lets through the same amount of light in half the time.

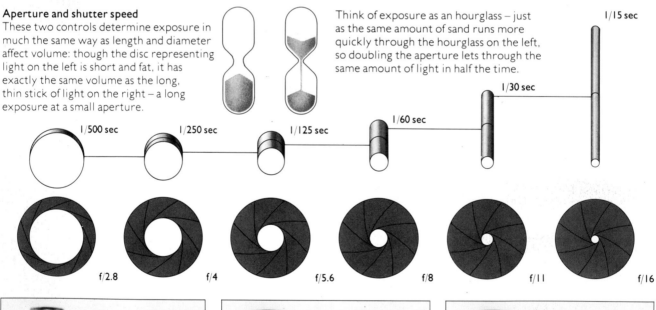

1/500 sec   1/250 sec   1/125 sec   1/60 sec   1/30 sec   1/15 sec

f/2.8   f/4   f/5.6   f/8   f/11   f/16

Wine splashing into a glass appears motionless at 1/500, but the brief exposure forces the use of a wide aperture, so there is little depth of field.

1/60 at f/8 is a good compromise – the film gets the same exposure, and the decanter is sharper, although the wine now shows signs of movement.

At f/16, the whole image is in focus, but getting correct exposure at this small aperture means using a speed of 1/15 – so the pouring wine is blurred.

Summer shadows cut a bold pattern of lines on the road, and draw your eye toward the car in the middle distance. The bright light gave the photographer plenty of freedom to choose shutter speed and aperture, so it was possible to keep the picture sharp from foreground to background by using a shutter speed of 1/250 and an aperture of f/11.

At a firework display there are far fewer choices – here the photographer needed a shutter speed of 1/125 to keep the group sharp, so he set the lens to its widest aperture to make the most of the dim light. He had to forgo depth of field.

Measuring light

Most modern cameras have some form of built-in light metering system that measures the brightness of the scene by means of light-sensitive cells, relates this to the film speed you have set, and either makes or recommends an appropriate exposure setting. When you point the camera at a subject and trigger the meter, a viewfinder display indicates which combination of shutter speed and aperture will provide a suitable exposure. The display may show actual settings or, by means of a moving needle or a flashing light-emitting diode (LED), guide you in adjusting settings. Some SLRs, and other versatile cameras, have through-the-lens (TTL) metering: cells inside the camera read the light after it has passed through the lens.

Meters indicate "correct" exposure as one that will record the subject in a mid-tone, between light and dark. The intention is to provide maximum detail, and an exposure suitable for most subjects. As a result, if you aim the camera at a sunlit wall the meter will select an exposure that will show the wall mid-grey in tone. If you point it at the same wall in deep shadow, the meter will recommend more exposure – again trying to show the wall mid-grey. Normally, however, in a scene of sun and shadow, the highlights are almost white, shady areas are dark and only some areas are mid-grey. Meters vary in the way they cope with this. They may simply average out the brightness of the whole image, but often they weight the average toward areas of the frame that are usually most important in pictures – the centre and lower half. Some allow "spot metering," taking the reading from a small central area of the viewfinder that you aim at the part of the image where you want most detail. The secret of successful exposure decisions is to understand how your particular meter reads a scene and to visualize in advance how you want the picture to look. No matter how sophisticated your camera, you alone can make the creative decisions.

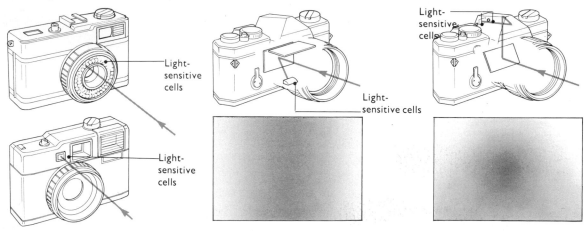

External metering (above)
Simple cameras incorporate the light-sensitive cells of the metering system either on the lens or in a window on the body to read reflected light.

TTL film plane metering (above)
Cells placed internally, near the film, read the actual light that forms the image, averaging the reading across the frame – with a slight central bias.

TTL centre-weighted metering (above)
Many systems give greater weight to the centre and lower half of the image in averaging the light reading. The cells are usually in the pentaprism.

Handheld meters allow more precise readings. The meter can be pointed at the subject, or from the subject back toward the camera itself. The meter's calculator dial then displays a choice of aperture and shutter combinations.

Understanding your meter
A centre-weighted meter gave perfect exposure for the skin tones opposite right, because the subject's face and arms filled the area of the frame given priority in this type of meter's system of averaging light. With a meter that measures light equally over the whole scene, this kind of shot is harder to get right. The bright sky behind the subject may influence the meter to indicate less exposure than the main subject needs. To avoid making errors you must know your own meter.

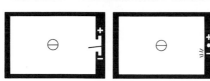

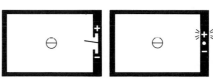

Underexposure
When the needle swings low, or the LED by the minus sign glows, the exposure is too little and the image too dark.

Correct exposure
When the needle is level, or the LED by the zero sign glows, the exposure is correct and detail will be good.

Overexposure
When the needle swings high, or the LED by the plus sign glows, the exposure is too great and the image too light.

Manual and automatic/1

The systems of measuring light built into cameras are designed to help you avoid making mistakes. They allow you to take pictures in a very wide range of lighting conditions with consistently accurate exposure. At the same time, there are great differences in the operation of cameras with through-the-lens metering, chiefly between manual and automatic models. There are even three separate types of "automatic exposure" cameras: fully automatic, aperture priority and shutter priority. Simple cameras may offer only one option but contemporary SLRs usually offer at least two – a priority system and a means of setting the exposure manually.

With fully automatic metering, the camera determines the exposure and sets both aperture and shutter. Complex electronics are involved, but operating these cameras is simple. On the other hand, you cannot vary the exposure, focus selectively, or control subject movement with shutter speed. Fully automatic cameras are thus more suited to snapshots than to creative picture taking.

The automatic systems relying on priority metering are much more flexible. You set either the shutter speed or aperture you require (depending on which of these two is given priority by the type of camera) and the camera then automatically sets the other control for correct exposure. This allows creative choice, yet frees you from making the final exposure setting so that you can concentrate on the subject. If the light changes at the last moment, the metering system makes the final adjustment.

Aperture priority, with which you set the f-number yourself, gives you control over depth of field and is helpful for landscapes, close-ups or other shots requiring great depth of field. Alternatively, you may want to use a large aperture to restrict depth of field deliberately.

Shutter priority gives you greater control of movement. You can set the shutter speed that will record a moving subject sharply – vital with action shots. With either type, you can in fact control both settings. With an aperture priority camera, for example, the shutter speed selected by the camera shows in the viewfinder display. Therefore, you can always adjust the aperture until, in compensation, the camera switches to the speed you want.

With manual exposure control, you can choose any combination you want, and you can even override the meter. This great flexibility and direct personal control can be very useful in unusual lighting situations and when you want a particular effect, such as the deliberate overexposure in the picture at right. Even if you do not always want to set the controls manually, a manual mode on an automatic camera is essential if you want to extend your range.

Aperture priority automatic

Set the aperture ring to the f-stop you want for depth of field, here f/11.

The camera then sets the speed and shows it on the viewfinder scale 1/125.

Shutter priority automatic

Set a shutter speed to control subject movement, here 1/250 on marker at left of dial.

The camera sets the f-stop and shows it at the top of the viewfinder display (f/8).

Manual control
Set either the f-stop or shutter speed and adjust the other control while looking through the viewfinder. In the viewfinder at right, the exposure is correct when a light glows next to the "0."

Creative control is needed with some subjects. Using a manual camera, the photographer could set the controls to overexpose the pavement and stop the little boy appearing as a silhouette.

Depth of field is important in the tranquil park scene above. The photographer wanted to show everything in sharp detail from the dappled foreground to the distant background figures. Aperture priority metering suits this type of scene.

Movement and timing are the crucial elements of the shot on the left. A fast shutter speed, and a quick response, have caught the flying spray and sense of fun perfectly. A shutter priority camera enabled the photographer to set the speed and then concentrate on the action.

Manual and automatic /2

When can you trust your camera meter, and when should you override it? If scenes with an average distribution of tones are lit from the front or the side, the camera's meter will probably serve well enough. But if the light is coming from behind the subject, for example, the meter may give a reading for the bright background so that the subject itself is underexposed and appears as a silhouette. Exposure often involves a creative decision and the meter's reading should be seen as a starting point. Identify the part of the scene you consider the main subject of the picture. If this is much lighter or darker than the rest, you should adjust the exposure to show good detail there, rather than accepting an average of the whole scene.

An effective way of basing exposure on the most important area is to take a "key reading" close to the main subject before moving back to your shooting position. You can do this readily with manual exposure controls but need some other method with automatic systems unless there is a so-called memory lock, which allows you to set the exposure and then hold it while you move to another camera position. Other automatic cameras have a compensation dial, which allows you to choose up to two stops more or less exposure than the automatically measured average of the scene.

Mixed light and dark areas in the same shot require care. If you think a light background such as the sky is biasing the meter, compensate by giving one or two stops extra exposure. Conversely, if you have a small, light subject against a dark background, give slightly less exposure than is indicated in case the meter is reading the background. For scenes with important detail in both light and dark areas, take readings for each and pick the midway setting. Averaging, as it is called, is useful for scenes with interesting skies or mixed sun and shade.

When you are in doubt, "bracketing" offers a solution. Take the same shot three or five times, changing the exposure in either one- or half-stop increments around the setting you think is correct.

Exposure compensation
Automatic cameras often have a dial for exposure adjustment. A light subject (right) may appear dull at the automatic exposure, but plus one stop on the dial restores the true brightness (far right).

Reading from a face

1 – When you need to set the exposure for an important element such as a face, move close so that the face fills the whole frame, and set the exposure.

2 – Then move back to your chosen camera position and take the shot at the same setting. Some automatic cameras have a memory lock to help you do this.

Bracketing is advisable when you are unsure of a reading. The meter alone could not determine the right balance in the scene below. The photographer made five varying exposures and selected the third frame as the best for enlargement.

1

2

3

4

5

Where should the light be?

Once you understand the fundamentals of setting exposure, you can forget the old rule about shooting with the sun behind the camera or over your shoulder. Although you should avoid strong light flaring directly into the lens, you can vary the camera's viewpoint in relation to the light, and achieve remarkable changes in appearance and mood of your pictures as a result.

The main thing is to try to choose the direction and quality of light that best suit the subject. If you are taking a portrait, for example, select an angle of light that allows the subject to look comfortably toward the camera, rather than squinting as the girl below right is doing. Move around and study the way shadows fall differently as your viewpoint

changes. And notice how the light models a subject to convey a sense of form – the three-dimensional aspect of things.

Frontlighting – light behind the camera – brings out good details and colour but tends to flatten form unless the light is soft. Side or oblique lighting is better for subjects with interesting textures – tree bark, for instance – or when you want to define features sharply, such as waves, rocks, or even a craggy face. Backlighting – light behind a subject – tends to conceal form altogether, especially if you expose for the background, turning the subject into a silhouette. The three landscapes on the opposite page show some of the transformations you can anticipate as the sun moves across the sky.

Strong sunlight forces the girl to shield her face with her hand (right) and screw up her eyes. Heavy shadows make her cheeks look gaunt. If you have to take shots of people in strong sun, try to avoid placing them so that they face into the full glare.

Using shade
You can take advantage of the soft light provided by the shade of an umbrella, building or tree when taking portraits. But remember to read the exposure directly from the face in case a bright or dark background fools the exposure meter.

Open shade offers far more flattering lighting (right). Here the light is even and diffused, softly modelling the girl's face and allowing her to relax her features and open her eyes. For this reason, an overcast day or soft evening light is good for portraiture.

Hard sidelighting from a bright morning sun casts long shadows and creates extreme contrast between the highlights and dense, featureless areas. The light shows up the knobbly texture of the ground and gives a powerful impression of the rugged terrain.

Nearly overhead sun in a hazy sky illuminates the top surfaces of the rocks, casting shorter and softer shadows. The broad light, diffused by the haze, gives strong modelling, revealing greater form and detail.

Backlit by a low sun, the horizon is etched against the evening sky. Detail is lost in all but the foreground crag, and shapes appear in delicate silhouette. The effect of the photograph is much more two-dimensional.

Handling limited light

Low light produces some of the most evocative and spectacular photographs you can take – from sunsets and dimly lit interiors to street scenes at night with illuminated signs and floodlit buildings. In order to use limited lighting effectively, you need first of all to escape from the idea that the only acceptable image is one that is evenly and brightly lit. At night or in a dark interior, for example, there is often too little light or too much contrast between highlights and shadows to obtain full detail over the whole image. Make a virtue of necessity, and take advantage of the way low light simplifies an image. You may be able to create a strong silhouette or take a shot in which the light forms an interesting rim around the subject. A good time to experiment is at dusk, when there is still enough light for a relatively short exposure, but street and house lights evoke a nocturnal mood.

To obtain enough light for exposure in low lighting situations, you often need to use both wide apertures and slow shutter speeds. You can shoot some subjects with a handheld camera if you have fast film and a lens with a wide maximum aperture – at least f/2.8. But many subjects demand a slow exposure, requiring a tripod or other form of camera support. When using a wide-angle or normal 50mm lens, support the camera for exposures slower than 1/60; with a long lens, 1/125 is about the slowest safe speed for handheld shots. One great advantage of a tripod and a long exposure is that you can use a very small aperture and so increase the overall sharpness of your image. However, very long exposures in dim light can produce unpredictable effects, especially with colour film, so you may need to try several different exposures to get the picture right.

Low light exposure guide
Exposure readings tend to be misleading in low light, but you can use this chart for typical subjects as a rough guide.

FILM IN USE	ISO 100		ISO 400	
Brightly lit shop windows	1/30	f/2.8	1/60	f/4
Well-lit street scenes	1/30	f/2	1/60	f/2.8
Fireworks	1/8	f/2.8	1/30	f/4
Floodlit buildings	2 secs	f/5.6	1/2	f/5.6
Street lights	1/4	f/2	1/15	f/2
Neon signs	1/30	f/4	1/125	f/4
Dim church interior	10 secs	f/4	2½ secs	f/4
Landscape at full moon	20 secs	f/2.8	5 secs	f/2.8

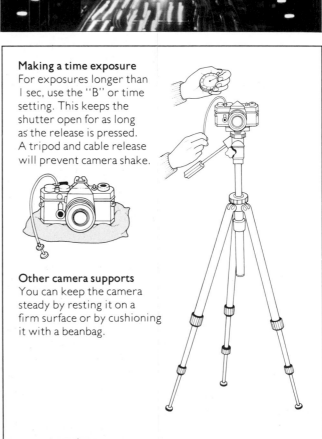

Making a time exposure
For exposures longer than I sec, use the "B" or time setting. This keeps the shutter open for as long as the release is pressed. A tripod and cable release will prevent camera shake.

Other camera supports
You can keep the camera steady by resting it on a firm surface or by cushioning it with a beanbag.

Snaking streaks of light (left) were created by a time exposure that recorded the head and tail lights of cars moving across the bridge. The evening sky provided the meter reading to show the bridge in silhouette.

Delicate rimlighting traces the monk's profile to produce a powerful portrait – the photographer metered the light on the monk's forehead, and gave one stop more exposure.

Shimmering water reflects light from the evening sun, backlighting the figures and foreground. To reduce the foreground to silhouettes, the photographer metered the bright area of water.

Using flash/I

The most portable and convenient means of providing extra light for photography is an electronic flash unit. At its simplest, the unit is about the size of a large matchbox, and has a gas-filled glass tube set in a reflector at the front. Sliding the unit into an accessory slot – known as the hot shoe – on top of the camera completes a circuit. And when you release the shutter, the circuit discharges a high voltage current between two electrodes in the tube, giving a brief, intense flash of light.

The speed of the flash – at least 1/500, and often much faster – is what really determines the length of the exposure. You need to adjust the shutter speed only to ensure that when the flash fires the entire frame is exposed. This usually means setting the shutter at 1/60 or slower to be sure that it is open fully when the flash fires. Because individual flash units vary in light output, they have a chart or dial showing which aperture to set on the lens and how far the light will reach. As explained below, sometimes you have a choice of apertures. On the simplest manual units you may need a different aperture for each different camera-to-subject distance. Some units automatically synchronize light output, aperture and shutter speed.

Between flashes, the unit recycles by drawing power from batteries and converting this to the high voltage capacitor charge needed to produce the next flash. As soon as the cycle of charging is finished – usually within five to ten seconds – a neon "ready" light comes on, indicating that there is enough power stored for another flash.

Power control

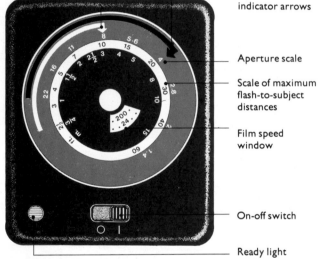

Aperture choice indicator arrows

Aperture scale

Scale of maximum flash-to-subject distances

Film speed window

On-off switch

Ready light

Using on-camera flash

The on-camera flash unit above has a calculator dial (enlarged above right) on its top surface. As an example, the dial has been set to show which f-stops you may choose if you are using ISO 200 film. You have a choice of f/4 or f/8 – the white and black arrows point to these f-numbers, and the maximum working distances appear alongside. In the operating sequence explained at the right, you select the correct power output with a switch elsewhere on the unit – again marked in white and black to correspond with the chosen aperture.

1 – Turn the calculator dial until the speed of the film in use appears in the window.

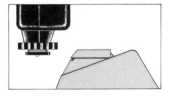

2 – Slide the foot of the flash unit into the camera's hot shoe.

3 – Set the shutter speed to 1/60 – sometimes marked with X or a lightning bolt.

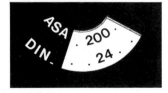

4 – Gauge the distance to the subject. Then choose the f-stop – here f/4 for 20 feet.

5 – Slide power control to the setting that corresponds with the aperture chosen.

6 – Switch on flash unit. You can take pictures soon after the ready light glows.

Simple electronic flash
Units such as the one at left are small enough to drop into a pocket, but can light subjects well only up to about 10 feet away.

Dedicated flash
The more powerful unit below left is matched – or dedicated – to a particular camera to reduce manual work. The reflector can tilt up to spread light.

High-power flash
The large unit at right has to be attached to the camera by means of a bracket. Two flash tubes give a greater output of light for difficult subjects and a cable connects the flash to the camera.

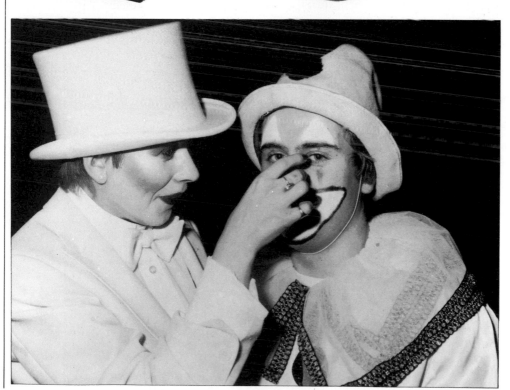

Random action – such as at a party – is a natural choice for a flash picture. The brief burst of light freezes all motion, and lights up only those parts of the subject closest to the camera, so that they stand out against a black background.

Using flash/2

An electronic flash unit is a highly useful source of light, but perched on top of the camera, pointing directly forward, much of its potential may be wasted. Pictures taken with the flash in the accessory shoe can look harsh and unnatural – portraits may appear unflattering, because flash, when it is aimed directly in line with the camera, seems to flatten the subject's features.

There are two ways of getting around this problem. The simplest is to move the flash off the accessory shoe, and hold it above or to one side of the camera. Most flash units have a short cable – called a flash cord – to make removal possible. The cord plugs into a small socket on the camera body, establishing an electrical connection so that the flash still fires at the moment of exposure.

In practice, the cord is often short, and you may have to buy an inexpensive extension cord, so that you can hold the flash at arm's length. To provide modelling illumination. point the flash straight toward the subject, but at an angle from the camera. It is easier to do this if you can get someone to hold the flash for you.

The other way to improve flash pictures is to bounce the light off a reflective surface such as a white-painted wall or ceiling. This method is more complicated than simply removing the flash from the camera, but it produces very soft, diffuse lighting that looks remarkably natural.

For correct exposure with bounce flash, you need a modern type of flash unit with a tilting reflector, and a photoelectric cell to measure and regulate the power of the flash automatically. When you tilt the reflector to point at the ceiling, this electric eye continues to point at the subject, and ensures that the unit provides enough power to compensate for light lost over the extra distance the light has to travel to the subject via the ceiling. Such a flash unit usually gives you several choices of aperture and you should always choose the widest aperture option for bounce flash. Used in this mode, the flash unit is operating at the limits of its power reserves, and choosing a small aperture may lead to underexposure. There is likewise a danger of underexposure with bounce flash – it is impractical in rooms with very high or dark-coloured ceilings.

Flash is useful not only in dark places but also in broad daylight. When the sun is very bright, the contrast between shadows and highlights may be excessive, so that the shadows look dark and murky. With a flash unit, you can fill in dark shadows with light, and brighten up the colours of the picture. Setting the exposure for fill-in flash is not quite as straightforward as for regular flash – the box on the opposite page explains how to do it.

Sparkling highlights give this impromptu portrait a party atmosphere. By taking the flash unit off the camera, the photographer was able to move the shadows to one side, and avoid the flat lighting that flash can produce when mounted on the camera.

Flash off the camera
Hold the flash at arm's length, and point it toward the subject. You need a long flash cord, and it helps if you have someone to hold the flash for you at an appropriate angle.

Fill-in flash

Bright sunlight, seemingly ideal for photography, can be very harsh – and particularly unflattering for portraits. When the sun is overhead or behind the subject, shadows can look empty and black.

An electronic flash unit can put light back into the shadows, as the pictures below show. But to retain the look of the natural light, you should reduce the flash power to about half its normal value.

You do this by "tricking" the flash into acting as though your film is more sensitive than it really is. On the unit's calculator dial, change the film speed setting so that it reads double the speed of the film you are using. This will give you a choice of smaller apertures. Pick the smallest and set this on the lens. (Simple units may not offer a choice.)

If you now take a meter reading, you may find that you can use the synchronized shutter speed, or slower, and still provide a correct natural light exposure. Finally, reduce the aperture by half a stop to adjust to the extra light from the flash.

Without flash

The natural look of the portrait above comes not from daylight but from bounce flash. With the flash unit pointed at the ceiling, the light reaching the subject is diffused, soft and even – perfect for portraits.

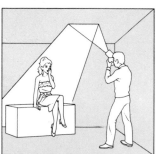

Bouncing flash

Choose the widest aperture the flash unit allows, and tilt the unit's head upward. This works best when the subject is close, and the ceiling or reflective surface is low and white.

With fill-in flash

STEPS TO BETTER PICTURES

Once you have mastered the basic practical control of your camera, you can concentrate on the creative techniques that lead to strong and interesting pictures. You may want also to explore the effects of changing lenses, or using filters to control colour and reflections. Adding to your equipment can improve results dramatically – a telephoto lens that lets you fill the frame with a single face really does add impact to a portrait, for example, and a wide-angle lens can enable you to take pictures that seem impossible. Extra lenses also introduce exciting opportunities for experiment – one of the great delights of photography is its ability to show us familiar objects in a new way. But sophisticated equipment is not enough. Learning how to exploit viewpoint, framing and timing, how to handle backgrounds, emphasize colours and shapes, portray movement or catch a split-second event – these are the techniques at the heart of successful picture-taking. Most of all, a photographer has to learn to select – a close-up of a flower can say more than a whole field of blooms. "Less is more" is a first principle of creative photography.

This close-up, front-on photograph of a maidenhair spleenwort fern highlights the delicacy of the plant. The composition has balance, the green of the plants seeming to flow down and through the layers of cool grey rocks. Lichen and moss add tone and texture to the image. A taste of the Pennines, one of the most beautiful regions in northern England.

Viewpoint

One of the simplest ways of achieving better pictures is to learn where to stand in relation to your subject and at what level or angle you should position the camera. Walk around looking at the subject through the viewfinder from different positions and angles. Think about whether you could improve the picture by moving closer, or standing farther back, or shooting from a low or high viewpoint. Simply moving the viewpoint in one of these ways can make the difference between a mundane picture and one that is truly striking.

Usually when you are photographing people, you should keep the camera level and point it directly at the subject. Even so, you should try different camera positions – to concentrate attention by moving in close, for example, or to include more of the surroundings by moving back. The choice may depend on whether you want to cut out a distracting background by moving in, or to add an interesting foreground with a longer view. Willingness to experiment will reveal many possibilities beyond the straightforward head-and-shoulders shot. Dramatically high or low viewpoints, or positions very close to the subject's face may just create ugly distortions. But provided the distortion is calculated, rather than an unwanted side-effect, there is no reason why you cannot succeed with an unusual approach.

With other subjects, your approach can be even freer. Buildings often look stunning when photographed from below, with the camera tilted steeply upward, and you can often bring out the pattern of city streets by shooting directly downward from a tall building. An ordinary tree could be intriguing seen from so close that only bark and a few leaves are in the frame. Whatever your subject and your intentions, try all the possibilities you can think of – and then look for more.

Classical columns tower over a low camera viewpoint. They make an imposing frame for the steel and glass grid of a modern building.

A highway from above becomes a dramatic diagonal composition of light and dark in the late afternoon sun. By using the vantage point of a high building and a downward camera angle, the photographer has found an image more exciting than the conventional city panorama would provide.

The sunbather could have been photographed from several different angles, and all of them would have been more obvious than the one chosen – standing directly over her and looking down. This was also the most effective, with blue water, white diving board, red wine, and tanned skin arranged in a striking composition.

A boy fixing his car grins at the photographer, who has joined him right down at ground level to make a charming, informal portrait. Inventive approaches such as this can produce outstanding shots, full of spontaneity and life. Technically, the shot is simplicity itself – using a standard lens on a 35mm camera in daylight.

How lenses control the image

In its ability to capture and focus the image of a subject on film, the lens is the most important part of the camera. The size and appearance of the image can vary greatly according to the type of lens you are using. And as all 35mm SLRs can be fitted with interchangeable lenses, photographers need to understand some basic lens characteristics.

How much of the scene a lens can capture depends on its angle of view – the way it sees the subject in front of the camera. This is determined by the focal length of the lens – in simple terms the distance from the optical centre of the lens to the film plane when focus is set to infinity. Focal length is marked on the front of the lens in millimetres, and this is how lenses are normally described – as 28mm, 50mm or 135mm lenses, for example. Most lenses are within a range from 18mm to about 600mm, although shorter and longer focal lengths can be obtained for more specialized purposes.

Lenses with short focal lengths can convey to the film more of a scene than the eye itself can see when looking through a frame the same size as the viewfinder. They do this by sharply bending the light passing through them, making each object in the scene appear smaller than the eye would see it and, by means of this optical shrinkage, fitting more objects into the frame. For this reason, lenses of short focal length are called wide-angle lenses. The most extreme of them is the so-called fisheye lens, which produces bizarre distortions by compressing an exceptionally wide view onto the relatively small format of the film. At the other end of the scale, telephoto lenses – with long focal lengths – bend the light from the subject relatively little, and produce an enlarged image of a small part of the view, as does a telescope.

From a single camera position, you can thus produce completely different views of the subject by

1 – A 28mm wide-angle lens takes in a broad view of the subject, but makes the distant buildings appear smaller than they would to the eye. This view of the Manhattan skyline from Liberty Island includes a large expanse of the stormy sky that loomed over the city when the shot was taken – and links near and far elements of the scene. But New York's famous skyline looks relatively insignificant.

2 – A 50mm normal lens renders the scene more as the eye would see it. The photographer aimed higher to keep in much of the sky but exclude the foreground. The lens helps to emphasize the city skyline, and the view is relatively wide.

using different lenses. With a wide-angle lens, a human figure can be shown as part of an extensive landscape, or you can close in on the face alone with a telephoto lens. The enormous flexibility gained by having interchangeable lenses is one of the great advantages of the 35mm SLR camera. On the other hand, individual lenses are expensive and also heavy to carry around. One solution is the zoom lens, which has a variable focal length, allowing you to achieve a range of framings and subject enlargements with a single lens. But be careful; good quality zooms are very expensive and they always have smaller maximum apertures than do equivalent lenses of fixed focal length. Zoom lenses are also heavier than lenses of fixed focal length because of their complex construction, and so may be more difficult to handle. The six pages that follow introduce the major types of lenses and the creative uses to which they can be put.

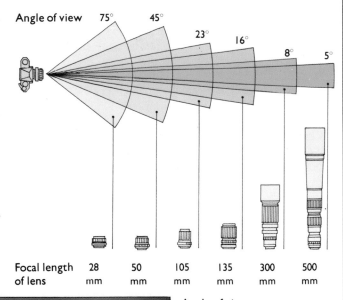

Angle of view	75°	45°	23°	16°	8°	5°
Focal length of lens	28 mm	50 mm	105 mm	135 mm	300 mm	500 mm

Angle of view
The lenses shown above with their angles of view are those most commonly used with 35mm SLRs. Note that the lens with the widest angle of view requires only a short body. Longer lenses can reach out farther to close in on (and enlarge) distant details. But as the focal length increases, the extent of the view decreases both in width and in height. Cameras with film formats larger than 35mm require lenses of longer focal length to achieve the same results, because more enlargement is needed to cover the larger area of the film itself.

3 – A 135mm telephoto lens brings forward the buildings in the same scene, making the twin towers of the World Trade Center the dominant subject. The sky now takes up a much smaller part of the frame, and the skyline is reduced in width.

75

The size we see

The 35mm SLR camera comes fitted with a 50mm lens (or sometimes 55mm) – the so-called normal lens. Many photographers never use any other lens, and still take perfectly good pictures.

The most striking feature of the image produced by a normal lens is the naturalness of its perspective. Because wide-angle lenses take in a broad view of the subject, they actually appear to reduce the scale of distant objects in relation to those in the foreground, thus exaggerating the perspective effect by which objects appear smaller the farther away they are. Telephoto lenses have the reverse effect, appearing to compress objects together despite the distance between them. The normal lens, on the other hand, reproduces the scene with its perspective much as the eye sees it. In a sense, photography is most objective with a normal lens – the camera shows the world essentially as we see it.

Because normal lenses are produced in large quantities, they are relatively cheap. They are also extremely versatile. They are suitable for near and distant subjects, accurately focusing subjects at a considerable distance and within two feet of the lens. And they can be used in low light – or with fast shutter speeds in action shots – because they have wide maximum apertures: f/1.8 is common and f/1.4 is not unusual. Taking good pictures with normal lenses needs skill, however. As there is no strong special photographic feature such as dramatic magnification to compensate for poor composition, the image can easily appear bland. More than with any other lens, you must frame the picture accurately and compose it carefully.

Street portraits look more natural when taken with a normal lens – the distortion-free images it forms closely resemble the world as seen with our eyes.

The normal lens
The photographer's workhorse, the 50mm or 55mm lens can give good definition, even in failing light.

A red bicycle, the same shade as the nearby door, establishes a simple but vibrant pattern of line and colour. For uncomplicated compositions such as this, the normal lens is ideal.

A tanned back says "summer sun" more eloquently than might a traditional beach scene. The close-focusing capability of the normal lens allowed the photographer to frame the image tightly and eliminate surrounding clutter.

Widening the view

Although a normal lens shows natural perspective, you need a lens of much shorter focal length to get breadth of view. The view of a normal lens is restricted to a viewing angle of about 45°, and to overcome this restriction, you need a lens that can fit more into the same frame – a wide-angle lens. With a standard SLR camera, any focal length shorter than about 35mm gives a wide-angle view, although the effects become really noticeable only at 28mm or shorter: many photographers use 35mm lenses in place of a normal lens. Focal lengths shorter than 24mm are available. But while compressing such a broad field of view onto the film format, very wide-angle lenses create distortion, and the more extreme of them are best considered as interesting

special-effects devices. Distortion will be most obvious with scenes involving straight lines, as in architectural photographs.

The most obvious practical use of a wide-angle lens is for pictures in which interesting details cover a wide angle in relation to where you are standing. If you want to show most of your living room in one photograph, for example, your eyes, with an angle of view approaching 160° from left to right, may see the whole room. But it may be impossible to move back far enough to fit everything into the viewfinder frame. A wide-angle lens will help by reducing the image of the objects in the room and squeezing more of them onto the film. In the same way, a wide-angle lens allows you to frame an exterior scene

Sweeping perspectives and an impressive sense of space give a dramatic look to landscapes shot with a wide-angle lens. Taking advantage of the distortion inherent in a 20mm lens, the photographer of the desert road on the left has turned his picture into a striking landscape, with the road itself forming a shape of startling impact.

Cramped space makes it impossible to move back far enough to show a subject like this adequately without a wide-angle lens. The 35mm lens used here was wide enough to allow the photographer to close in on a furniture restorer and the instrument he is polishing, yet still show his surroundings.

Framed by an arch, and shaded by citrus trees, these Portuguese women make a fascinating folk tableau for the camera. By composing the picture in order to exploit the wide angle of view and great depth of field of the 28mm lens he was using, the photographer was able to include much of the surroundings, and to identify the location as a quiet courtyard. A normal lens would have shown only the group, losing much of the intimacy of this image.

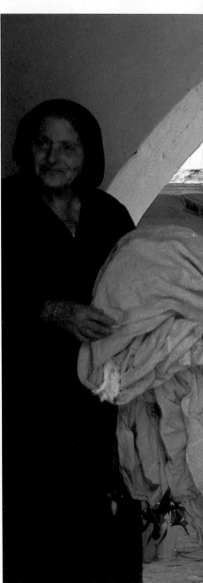

effectively with foreground objects near the frame edges, as in the shot here taken through an archway. The result is often to draw the viewer into the picture, creating a feeling of involvement that can give photographs taken with a wide-angle lens a strong sense of immediacy.

As a most useful side-effect, lenses of short focal length produce greater depth of field than do normal lenses at the same aperture. This makes them very useful in poor light and in situations where there is little time to make fine adjustments to the focus. When you are photographing general street scenes, for example, a wide-angle lens will let you point the camera and shoot without delaying to adjust the focusing ring.

24mm

28mm

35mm

Wide-angle lenses
These three lenses, which have focal lengths of 24mm, 28mm and 35mm, outwardly resemble normal lenses. But the likeness ends as soon as you fit one to your camera and look through the viewfinder. Cramped views expand, and at small apertures the depth of field makes focusing less critical.

Concentrating the view

Distant subjects that look good in the viewfinder often seem disappointing in the final print, because the attractive details that initially caught the eye occupy only a small area in the middle of the frame. Moving closer is sometimes the answer, but if you are photographing a football game, for example, you cannot intrude on to the playing area. The solution is to use a telephoto lens. This has an effect opposite to that of a wide-angle lens – instead of taking in a wider field of view than a normal lens, it records a much smaller area, and magnifies the subject.

The degree of magnification depends on the focal length of the lens. A 100mm telephoto has a focal length double that of a normal lens, so it doubles the scale at which the eye would perceive a subject. At the same time, the lens's horizontal field of view is half as wide as that of a standard lens.

The most popular telephotos have focal lengths of between 85 and 250mm. The longer focal lengths, although powerful, are much more difficult to handle and to focus. Those of 400mm and longer can pick out subject details missed by the naked eye but require tripod support.

Besides their magnifying effect, all telephoto lenses have several other common characteristics. The most dramatic of these is the compression of distance that they appear to cause. If you look at a row of objects of equal height and equally spaced – such as telegraph poles – receding into the distance, you will notice that the distant ones seem more tightly packed. When you photograph this scene with a telephoto lens, only the distant poles are included in the frame, and so the picture appears flattened out with its different planes packed together. For example, in the shot of the Grand Canyon on the opposite page, a scene that stretches away from the camera for several miles has been foreshortened startlingly, because a long lens has eliminated the foreground.

Another important characteristic of a telephoto lens is that it gives less depth of field than does a normal lens. As a result, when the lens is focused on a nearby object, the background is unsharp – a useful way of concentrating attention on the principal area of interest. Portraiture with telephoto lenses is often effective for this reason – and also because you do not need to crowd your subject to get a detailed head-and-shoulders shot.

Telephoto lenses

Telephoto lenses magnify the image, filling the frame with a subject that may look like an insignificant detail when seen through a normal lens. These three lenses have focal lengths of 135mm, 200mm and 400mm, magnifying the image 2.7, 4 and 8 times respectively.

200mm

400mm

135mm

Pleasing portraits are easier with a telephoto – its shallow depth of field puts background distractions out of focus. At the same time, magnification of the image allows you to move back to a more comfortable working distance, thus eliminating perspective distortions.

The majesty of landscape is often missing from pictures taken with a normal lens. A telephoto can restore the sense of scale and drama – as in the picture here of the Grand Canyon, taken with a 200mm lens.

The thick of the action at a sports event usually can be captured effectively only with a telephoto lens. The photographer of the football game opposite used a 400mm lens to get close to a player weaving through tacklers on the far side of the field.

Recording everything sharply

More often than not you will want your entire image to be sharp from foreground to background – to give a figure a sense of location, for example, to link foreground and background elements, or merely to record the whole of a view. The simplest way to maximize depth of field is to stop down the lens. Stopping down means reducing the aperture of the lens, and the smaller the aperture you use, the greater the depth of field in your photograph. Stopped down to f/16, for example, a normal lens focused on a subject 15 feet away will record sharply everything beyond about eight feet, whereas with the aperture widened to f/2, only the subject itself will be sharply focused, the background and foreground appearing blurred.

Stopping down the lens requires that you also slow the shutter speed to give sufficient exposure. Unless the light is bright, this may limit your freedom to choose an aperture small enough to gain the depth of field you want. Fast film can help or, if the subject is static, you may be able to shoot at a slow shutter speed with the camera steadied – preferably on a tripod. To check how much of your picture will be sharp at a given aperture, you can either refer to the depth of field scale on the lens (see below left) or use the preview button. This closes the lens down to the f-stop you have chosen, allowing you to see through the viewfinder the zone of sharp focus in your image.

Two other factors control the extent to which you can record the whole picture sharply – the lens you use and the camera-to-subject distance. The shorter the focal length of your lens the greater the depth of field. Thus a wide-angle lens has advantages if you want the greatest near-to-far sharpness. Finally, you can extend sharpness by moving back from your subject, since depth of field increases with the distance between the camera and the subject.

Using the depth of field scale
A typical lens (below) has a focusing distance scale linked by engraved lines to pairs of f-numbers on a depth of field scale. From a chosen f-number, the left-hand line indicates the distance to the nearest point in sharp focus and the right-hand line indicates the farthest point.

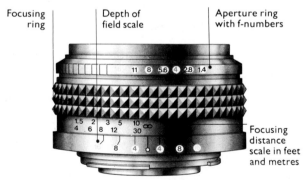

Above, the lens is focused on infinity (marked with a ∞ symbol on the distance scale) and the aperture set at f/8. The line from the "8" on the left points to 16 feet, showing that focus is sharp only beyond about 5 metres. The "8" line on the right, which is well beyond the infinity symbol, indicates that there is depth of field to spare.

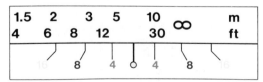

By turning the focusing ring to the right so that the ∞ symbol aligns with the "8" line on the right, infinity is still in focus. But depth of field now extends down to 10 feet, so more of the foreground is in focus.

The maternal bond between an ostrich and her eggs makes a striking composition. Focusing on the midground ensured that both were sharp despite the distance dividing them.

Isolating what is important

In photography, you often need to take special measures to focus attention on one centre of interest – usually because there are distracting elements in front of or behind your main subject, and you may not be able to get near enough to your subject to cut out the unwanted details. When you are taking a candid portrait, for example, bright colours or strong shapes in the background or foreground may compete for attention with your chosen subject. In such circumstances the best way to simplify the image is to put intrusive elements out of focus by deliberately creating a shallow depth of field. Colours are toned down and shapes reduced to an unobtrusive blur when they are out of focus.

There are three ways of minimizing depth of field: using a wide aperture, a long-focus lens or a close viewpoint. Just as you can stop down the lens to achieve maximum depth of field (overleaf), so you can deliberately open up the lens and choose the widest aperture possible to take advantage of the restricted focus it offers. Of course, using a wide aperture makes it crucial that you focus accurately on the part of the scene you want to be sharp, as any slight error will be noticeable. Because long-focus lenses have more limited depth of field than normal lenses, they are well suited for selective focusing, especially when set at a wide aperture. Finally, if the light is too bright for a very wide aperture to be feasible, remember that you can also throw a background out of focus by moving in close to your subject – depth of field is shallower in close-ups than at average focusing distances.

A face in a crowd can be made to stand out. Here, the photographer focused carefully on the girl, then opened up the lens to blur the foreground leaves and soften the background. The blurred elements serve both to emphasize the sharply focused face and to frame it.

Zoo portraits are often spoiled by cage bars and wire netting. Here, however, the photographer concentrated attention on the main subject by holding the camera close to the cage and using a wide aperture to cut depth of field. This throws the bars and netting so out of focus that they are almost imperceptible.

A girl balancing on the bar of her sports bicycle totally dominates the picture here, because a long-focus lens set at a wide aperture has been used in order to soften the intrusive colours and shapes in the busy street behind her. Shooting with a long-focus lens is also a simple way of filling the frame with your main subject without having to get too close.

Moving subjects/1

The camera's ability to capture a permanent image of momentary events and moving objects is one of the most persuasive charms of photography. The shutter makes this possible: its fastest speeds enable you to halt a thundering express train, or transfix in mid-air a child on a swing. Often, however, lighting conditions oblige you to use shutter speeds slower than the ideal for stopping action. In these circumstances you need to know how slow a speed you can safely use without the subject appearing as a formless blur. The choice you make may depend on several factors.

An obvious consideration is how fast the subject is moving; but much more important is the rate at which the subject's image is passing across the film. This depends on distance and direction. When the subject is far off, or is either approaching you head-on or going away from you, the image is changing its position more slowly on the film than when the subject is nearby and crossing the frame. You can therefore use a slower shutter speed if you want to freeze the movement of distant, approaching or receding subjects.

Composing the picture so that distance and direction are working for you is one way to make maximum use of the camera's action-stopping power. Another trick is to exploit natural pauses in otherwise rapid movements. Many moving subjects actually reach equilibrium for brief instants: a pole-vaulter, for example, is almost static for a moment before dropping over the bar. By anticipating this peak in the action, you can give the illusion of freezing fast movement even when you are obliged to use a slow shutter speed. The picture on this page of a girl on a swing was taken in just this way: the photographer waited until she was almost motionless in the air, then pressed the shutter.

To capture the excitement of a splash in the surf, the photographer set a fast shutter speed of 1/1000 sec. Not only has this frozen the girls' flailing legs; it has even recorded the water as a shimmering cascade of crystal drops.

Swinging high in the air, this little girl reaches an instant of equilibrium at the end of each arc. At these moments, even quite slow shutter speeds can produce crisp images that seem to sum up the rapid movement in between.

Shutter speeds to freeze movement
The chart at the right indicates the shutter speeds needed to stop movement in a range of subjects at progressively greater distances from the camera. The walker could be stopped at 1/125 from nearby, but the cyclist would need to be 30 yards away and the car and train even farther. For safety, shoot fast if a subject is crossing the frame.

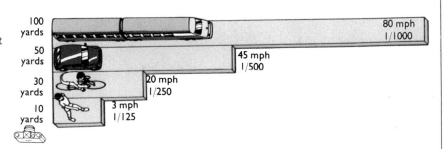

100 yards
50 yards
30 yards
10 yards

80 mph
1/1000
45 mph
1/500
20 mph
1/250
3 mph
1/125

Moving subjects/2

In recording a crisp, sharp image of a moving subject, a fast shutter speed may fail to give a true impression of motion. Setting a shutter speed that is too slow to freeze all movement results in an image that is slightly blurred. But this image may come much closer to the way we perceive speed – as a continuous flow of motion. In the pictures here, for example, whirling or blurred lines give a vivid sense of movement. Such pictures often work best if only part of the subject is blurred while the rest of the image is sharp and clear in the normal way. The trick is to choose a shutter speed that will give enough blur to suggest motion yet not so much that the subject is unrecognizable. This is easiest when elements of the subject move at different speeds, as in the shot below of the galloping horse, where the pounding hooves are blurred although the horse's head and body retain their shapes.

A less obvious but highly effective way of suggesting movement is to move the camera itself so that static parts of the subject are blurred, just as they appear when we are moving ourselves. The streaks around the car and driver on the opposite page were produced by the camera technique known as panning. With the shutter set to a slow speed of 1/60, the photographer simply pivoted his body so as to keep the moving subject in the centre of the frame throughout the exposure. The panning blurs the background (or foreground) but keeps the subject sharp and clear. You will need some practice to select the optimum shutter speed (1/30 to 1/125 is generally a sensible choice for most subjects) and also to achieve a smooth pan with the subject centred. You should try to choose a subject lighter in colour or tone than the background against which it is moving, although the blue Bugatti is effective.

The speeding Bugatti is sandwiched between streaks of non-specific countryside, actually grass fields and trees beyond. By panning the camera, the photographer has caught perfectly the tension and concentration of the driver while blurring the stationary scene around, conveying something of the speed and excitement of the racing car.

Animal energy seems to flow from the image of a galloping Arab stallion. A fast shutter speed could have defined the horse more clearly but would probably have given a less vivid sensation of motion than does this impressionistic picture. The camera was panned at 1/60 to keep pace with the horse but not with its flying hooves.

Like spinning tops, the full skirts of these Spanish dancers leave a whirling trace on the film. A slow shutter – 1/15 – softens the dancers' outlines but sharply records the spectators at the edge of the stage.

The hurtling momentum of machines allows you to use fairly fast shutter speeds and still suggest motion. For the dusk shot of a fairground, the photographer chose a shutter speed of 1/125.

Anticipating the moment

Nearly all photography needs an alert sense of timing. This means being able to respond instinctively to the image in the viewfinder, so that you release the shutter at the best possible moment. But, to be sure of taking consistently good pictures, you also need anticipation and planning, especially with action photographs.

The faster the subject is moving, the more preparation becomes essential. The explosiveness of most sports, for example, means that you need to work out your shots before the action starts. At a horse race, you might decide that the instant of maximum visual energy will occur just as the horses burst from the starting gates. To capture it you will need to line up the viewfinder on the gate, carefully select the framing, and preset both focus and exposure. Then, when the moment you saw in your mind's eye arrives, you will not be left fumbling with the controls. Some action shots – such as the picture of a hurdler below – are not possible without planning, no matter how fast the photographer's reactions are.

Anticipating the best moment for a shot can be equally important with more static subjects, such as landscapes or buildings, because of the way the changing light affects their appearance and mood. If possible, observe your subject at different times of day, or try to imagine the scene with the sun in different positions in the sky. The castle buildings opposite, for example, are far more impressive thrown into relief by a low sun than they would have looked an hour earlier.

With the chance to plan a photograph, the best angle and most effective moment can be chosen for taking a shot. The low vantage point has thrown the substantial buildings of Eilean Donnan Castle into stark relief against the evening sky, seen at its best as the sun nears the horizon. The moody effect is completed by the reflection of the castle in the water and the distant haze of the island beyond. Located in the Scottish Highlands, close to the Isle of Skye, the castle is just one of many picturesque landmarks in the region.

Planning, anticipation, and split-second timing were needed to catch the hurdler at this dramatic moment. Before the race began, the photographer selected one particular runner and set the focus on one of the hurdles he would cross. With the exposure controls also preset, the shutter was fired at the moment the approaching athlete came into sharp focus above the hurdle.

cantabrian

Closing in

Taking photographs at close range reveals a world that usually goes unnoticed – a world full of delicate patterns, beautiful colours and textures. Apart from the wealth of natural subjects – rocks, shells, fruits, flowers or insects – many man-made objects that would look dull when shot at a normal scale become startling when isolated in close-up. With a normal 50mm lens you can focus as close as about 18 inches, and this is generally sufficient for most photographic situations. But if you are shooting a very small subject, such as a flower or an insect, even with the lens at its minimum focusing distance you will be unable to fill the frame with it and show every small detail. For this you need a special type of lens called a macro lens or some form of close-up attachment (as shown below) that allows you to focus closer to your subject and thus obtain a larger and more detailed image of it on the film.

Most close-up equipment works on the same basic principle – it moves the lens farther away from the film, to bring very close objects into focus and magnify the image. In the process, the brightness of the image decreases, as light has to travel farther to reach the film. And this, in turn, affects exposure. A camera with through-the-lens metering will indicate the adjusted exposure necessary. Otherwise, and if the close-up attachment you are using does not couple the lens diaphragm to the camera body, you must make extra exposure calculations.

Precise focusing is crucial when you are working close up, as depth of field is extremely shallow – in some cases no more than a few millimetres. Often you can take advantage of this limitation to emphasize the centre of interest. But to obtain a sharp image of the whole of a small subject, you will have to choose a viewpoint that requires least depth of field, and select the smallest aperture possible. This means either mounting the camera on a tripod for a long exposure or using flash to supply more light. When you take pictures of flowers or insects in their natural habitat, flash is generally the best solution, since it will freeze movement, as well as bring out bright colours. If lighting conditions permit, try to use fairly slow film for close-up work, because the graininess of fast film may obscure fine detail you want to record.

Close-up equipment

A macro lens can be used for both ordinary shots and close-ups, since it can focus on subjects from infinity down to a few inches away. It performs best at very close range.

Supplementary lenses that screw onto the front of the lens are available in varying strengths. They do not cut down the light, and several can be added to obtain greater magnification.

Extension tubes can be fitted to move the lens farther from the focal plane and permit closer focusing. They cost little, come in varying lengths, and can be added to record images of small objects at life size.

Bellows units fitted between camera body and lens permit continuous adjustments of focus, unlike the rigid tubes. They cost more but also magnify more, because they stretch the lens farther out from the camera body.

Old boots and gloves may seem an unlikely subject, but close framing of such everyday objects forces the viewer to see them anew, often with pleasure.

The crisp outline of a butterfly stands out clearly against the muted background. When you are working close up, you can more easily keep subjects in sharp focus if they are spread out along a fairly flat plane.

The intricate patterns of the natural world may need the extra magnification of close-up equipment to do them justice. Notice the way that the minimal depth of field results in only the near side of the horse chestnuts being in focus, with the far side blurred.

Using simple filters

Sometimes you can improve your pictures by using filters to change, control or partly block light entering the lens. Although this may sound complicated, filters are just thin sheets of glass, gelatin or plastic that either screw onto the lens front or slip into special holders in the same position.

The filters that are used most often are those that clean up the light from the subject. Skylight or ultraviolet (UV) filters absorb ultraviolet radiation, which can make distant objects appear hazy, particularly when conditions are very bright. Use them in conjunction with a lens hood, which will help to exclude the stray light that sometimes reaches the lens, causing flare and softening the image.

In some circumstances, a polarizing filter can produce even more useful effects. This filter can cut down glare from the sky, from water, from glass or other reflective surfaces. Light travelling from these surfaces often becomes polarized, which means that it vibrates mainly in one plane instead of at all angles perpendicular to its line of direction. By blocking the polarized plane, the filter gives a sharper image, and will attractively darken a blue sky.

Another important group of filters absorbs specific colours. A pale yellow filter, for example, passes red and green light but blocks blue. Because this leaves the blue areas underexposed, yellow filters can be used in black-and-white photography to darken the sky and make clouds stand out boldly. With colour film, however, every part of the scene will be subtly tinted toward the colour of the filter you use. The yellowish series of filters widely known by the Kodak serial number 81, for example, can be used to impart a general warm tint.

You can also buy a great variety of special effects filters. The colour effects of some of these are shown in Part Two of this book on pages 196-200.

No filter

With polarizing filter

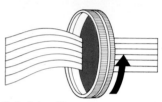

Polarizing filter
This type of filter helps to cut unwanted glare. Rotate the filter's ring until the image in the viewfinder darkens.

The startling difference between the two pictures of prehistoric rock engravings in Utah (above) shows the ability of a polarizing filter to reveal detail that would otherwise be hidden by glare. Polarizing filters also have the effect of darkening blue skies, as in the atmospheric picture of trees (below), and can often enliven landscapes.

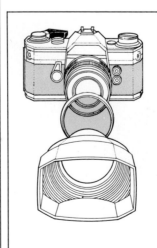

UV filter and lens hood
An ultraviolet filter attached permanently to the lens will improve your outdoor pictures and protect the delicate front of the lens. Lens hoods should frame the picture area closely. Square types such as the one at left with modified corners do this most effectively. They are particularly suited to wide-angle lenses, because circular hoods sometimes cut off the corners of the image at wide apertures.

A soft, misty look can be
introduced with a diffusion
filter as in the romantic
image of the flowers in the
picture at far right.

The seascape below has
been improved by a graduated
filter that darkens part of the
image. Without the filter, the
sky would have appeared as
an empty area of white. The
filter contributes the colour.

Recognizing patterns and outlines

The world is rich in bold outlines and rhythmic patterns that have strong visual attractions when they are isolated and emphasized in photographs. Finding them is largely a matter of forgetting for the moment that you are looking at things in a literal way – as trees, buildings or individual people – and trying to see the underlying design of the picture in your viewfinder. Learning to see patterns and outlines will help you to produce less haphazard photographs even when these more abstract visual qualities are not the main point of the picture.

Patterns are everywhere, and the camera's ability to close in on the most significant parts of a scene enables you to accentuate such patterns by framing the shot to exclude more random elements. Similarly, you can emphasize patterns by viewpoint and camera angle, as in the picture of the windmill on the opposite page, for which the photographer took up a position that stresses the lines of planking.

Outlines are somewhat harder to recognize, because in the real world we do not usually see things in terms of flat areas of shape or colour, except when they are silhouetted. But photography has a particular capacity to transcribe the three-dimensional world in terms of basic outlines – especially when light is coming from behind the subject. You can produce simple, forceful pictures by deliberately placing the subject between you and the light and choosing an exposure for the background rather than for the immediate subject. For best results, there should be a difference of at least three stops on your meter scale between subject and background. Alternatively, shapes can be emphasized by contrasting a light subject against a dark background, or a shape of one colour against a plain background of another hue.

A windmill becomes a graphic pattern of rushing lines, which almost conceal the true identity of the subject. The photographer took full advantage of the bright sunlight to emphasize shadows, forming solid black lines between the boards and throwing the back of the mill into darkness.

The random patterns of nature can easily be vividly emphasized. For this photo of a barnacle-encrusted rock, the photographer moved in close in order to exclude the surroundings, and framed an attractive pattern that is reminiscent of a modern abstract painting.

Backlit in a deck chair, the nude girl (left) appears as a bold, near-silhouetted shape, reflected intriguingly in the shallow water. The photographer had set the exposure for the lighter background so that the girl herself would appear as a dark, outlined shape with little visible detail.

THE MAGIC OF COLOUR

Colours can be breathtaking when their impact is concentrated within the frame of a photograph – deep and resonant reds, subtly modulated greens, singing yellows, solemn or brilliant blues. Although the foundations and traditions of photography were laid in black and white, few photographers today can resist the power of colour to evoke excitement, impact, variety – and simply to delight the eye.

There is, of course, a whole range of photographs in which colour may be no more than an incidental element, subsidiary to the main point – which may be to record an event, or an aspect of human behaviour, or the expression on a single face. However, this part of the book specifically explores the way you can make colour itself the subject of the picture by using it purposefully rather than incidentally. Developing this ability to use colour creatively can be an absorbing adventure, which may change your whole attitude to colour and make you aware that its influence is emotional as well as visual. Colour has its own eloquence. The pictures on the following eleven pages work as they do because colour is the essential element. Imagine, as you turn the pages, how much would be lost if the images were in black and white. This is the magic of colour.

Autumn colours billow in a soft wave over the little girl playing in a park. The picture's charm stems largely from the photographer's decision to allow the beauty of the tree's colours to fill most of the frame.

Red boat, blue water, *join in a curve of richly saturated colour. Such images speak to us simply. The photographer needed only to spot the freshly painted boat and frame it closely to relate the strong red to the blue of the sky reflected in the clear water.*

The beauty of a woman,
her smile, and her patterned
sweater are brought out by
a setting that reveals the
photographer's eye for the
way colours work together.
The vivid red background
and the frame of dark bricks
complement perfectly the
subtle hues of the sweater.

Pale balloons *float against a sombre background of shadowed architecture in a composition that deliberately restricts colour to a small area of the frame. The surprising impact of the picture demonstrates the power of colour to sway us with the lightest touch.*

Interlocking segments
*of solid colour turn a hillside
into an abstract pattern that
suggests the strength of the
landscape itself. The picture
has been carefully exposed
and printed to heighten the
contrasting tones of the
sky and hill against the
thin yellow line of crops.*

Lily pads, *curving grasses, and the glassy surface of a pond create cool colour harmonies that only an observant eye might notice. By moving in close, you can often discover such hidden beauty in nature and isolate it in pictures.*

Beach umbrellas, *abandoned during a rain shower, sweep in a delicate green arc across the whole picture. The blending and softening of hues on a misty day such as this often creates marvellous opportunities for colour photographs.*

Windblown barley has
been blurred here by the
choice of a shutter speed too
slow to stop the tips of the
stalks waving. By this means
the photographer has subtly
muted the overall colour
to pale green.

A motorcycle racer banks over to take a corner, the bright red of the rider's suit standing out against the dark of the track. The photographer used a special prism filter to create the repeated image that gives such a dramatic impression of high speed.

COLOUR AND COLOUR FILMS

One of the most fascinating things about colour photography is the enormous range of colour effects that can appear in your pictures. Very often, colours do not turn out the way you expected – they may be stronger or duller than you remembered them, or there may be an overall tinge of a single colour, of which you were not aware when you took the picture. However, this unpredictable quality is not really so surprising: colour photography involves a delicate relationship between the colours of objects, the colours of light, and those of colour films.

The section that follows begins by looking at the source of all colours – light itself. Because direct sunlight at midday combines all the colours of the spectrum, the illumination it provides may appear colourless. But other light sources, such as light bulbs – and sunlight itself at evening or in the morning – have a definite bias toward orange or red. A person's face can look quite a different colour depending on the quality of the prevailing light. Films are highly sensitive to these colour differences. Moreover, various types and brands of films differ in the emphasis they give to some colours at the expense of others.

To achieve the best results in colour photography, you need to make sure you are using the film most suited to the type of lighting. A few slide films are designed specially for use in the orange light of tungsten studio lamps. Alternatively, you may be able to modify the light passing through the lens by using a filter. The ability to control precisely the colours that appear in your pictures is the first step toward using colour creatively.

A rainbow in the fine spray falling from an overhead fire hose reveals the colours making up the sunlight flooding a Pittsburgh street scene. Although the colours of light are seldom seen so clearly, everything in the world owes its colour to the light that illuminates it.

Light and colour vision

To understand why we see the world in a variety of colours, you need first of all to look at the nature of light itself. Like X-rays or radio waves, light is one of the forms of electromagnetic energy that radiates in waves from energy sources such as the sun – somewhat as rings spread out from a pebble thrown into a pond. The essential difference between the light falling on this page and the signals picked up by a radio or television set is one of wavelength – the distance from the crest of one wave to the crest of the next. In some forms of energy the wavelength is infinitesimal – no more than a billionth of a milli-

metre; in others it can be as much as ten kilometres. The wavelengths of visible light are around 1/2000th of a millimetre.

For the photographer, the important difference between light and any other form of radiant energy is the fact that we can see it. Out of all the wavelengths of energy radiating through the atmosphere, the nerve endings in our eyes are sensitive to only a narrow band that constitutes the visible spectrum, diagrammed below. The ultraviolet and infra-red wavelengths on either side of this band are invisible to our eyes. The eye and the brain assign different

How we perceive the colours of light

The large diagram below graphically simplifies a complex process by which we see colours in the light radiating from the sun. Light itself forms only a tiny band of wavelengths among other forms of energy spreading out in intermingled waves of widely differing lengths. Yet the relatively narrow band of visible wavelengths provides our whole multicoloured world of light. When a prism splits light into its individual wavelengths we can see a spectrum of colours, as in the photograph at right. And, remarkably, we see this by interpreting signals from just three types of cells in the retina, sensitive to wavelengths of red, green or blue light, enabling us to perceive a myriad different hues.

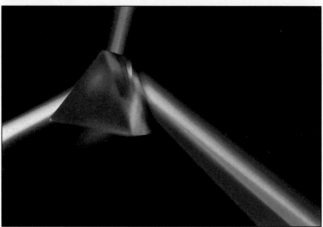

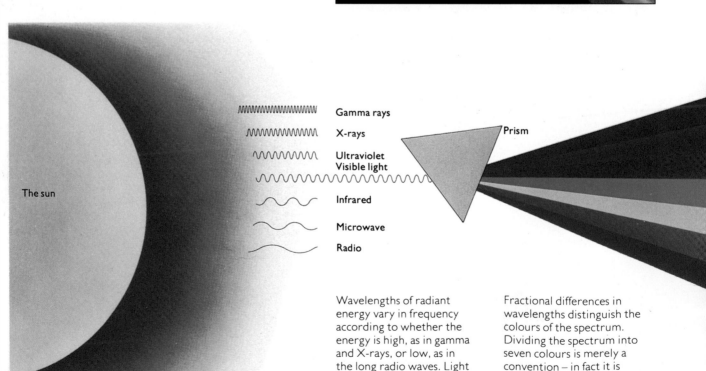

The sun

Gamma rays
X-rays
Ultraviolet
Visible light
Infrared
Microwave
Radio

Prism

Wavelengths of radiant energy vary in frequency according to whether the energy is high, as in gamma and X-rays, or low, as in the long radio waves. Light is simply another form of energy, of medium wavelength.

Fractional differences in wavelengths distinguish the colours of the spectrum. Dividing the spectrum into seven colours is merely a convention – in fact it is a continuous band, made up of numberless hues.

hues to those wavelengths to which they are sensitive, interpreting the longest of them as red and the shortest as violet. In daylight, the wavelengths that make up the visible spectrum are complete, mixing together in such a way that the light appears white, or colourless. But a rainbow reveals the fact that the light actually contains all the spectrum colours, because the droplets of water break apart the individual hues. You can separate the colours of the spectrum simply by passing a beam of white light through a prism, as shown below. And by using a filter to take out one or more of the colours, you can make the light itself look coloured rather than white. For example, a blue filter absorbs red and green lightwaves, allowing only blue to pass.

The reason that we see the world in a multitude of colours is mainly because different substances and surfaces absorb certain wavelengths of light and reflect others back to the eye. The eye then reads the reflected light in terms of the predominant wavelengths, and assigns a hue to it. Thus a tree looks green and a poppy red because they absorb and reflect different wavelengths of the light that shines on them both.

Soap bubbles, like the prism, bring out the colours in white light (right). The surface of a bubble varies in thickness and passes or reflects different colours of light accordingly. The result is a shimmering pattern of shifting colours.

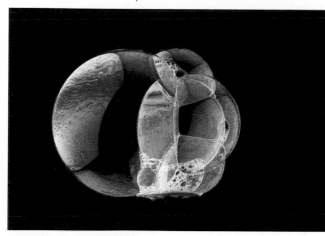

Why objects look coloured
When rays of light fall on a surface, wavelengths of some colours are absorbed, others reflected. Those reflected back to the eye determine how we perceive an object's colour (below).

Here the ball looks red because only wavelengths we perceive as red are reflected: all the other wavelengths are absorbed.

When wavelengths of more than one primary colour are reflected back (such as red and green), they create a new colour (here, brown).

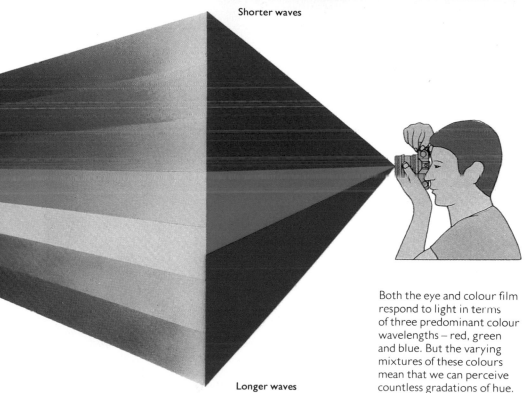

Shorter waves

Longer waves

Both the eye and colour film respond to light in terms of three predominant colour wavelengths – red, green and blue. But the varying mixtures of these colours mean that we can perceive countless gradations of hue.

If an object reflects all the spectrum's wavelengths and absorbs none, it will appear to be coloured white, as does this ball.

The balance of colour/I

The sun, a candle and a glowing coal all give off light as they release heat. But the colour of the light that each produces is not identical, because the heat at which each source burns varies enormously. As a result, each source sends out a different mixture of wavelengths, with substantial effects on the colours of the objects illuminated. These effects are particularly noticeable in colour photographs because films are balanced to give accurate colours in light of a particular wavelength mixture.

There is no point in relying on your eyes to detect minor changes in lighting. We see what we expect to see, ignoring subtle variations of colour. A white shirt will still look white to us whether we see it in sunlight or indoors under artificial light. However, film records the predominant colour of the lighting literally. Ordinary film for daylight use is balanced for average noon light in which the illumination comes mainly from the predominantly white light of the direct sun. Unless you correct it with a filter, lighting of a very different balance will inevitably change the colours in photographs taken with this same film, producing unreal colours – an effect known as a colour cast.

The colour of a light source does not depend only on its heat. For example, atmospheric factors come into play when we consider the way daylight changes in colour. As a result, whereas daylight or noon sun appears neutral, the wavelength mixture reaching us varies as the sun rises or sets. Similarly, clouds or haze filter out some wavelengths by absorption, or scatter others so that they predominate in the light reflected from the sky itself. On a clear day, the sky looks intensely blue because of the scattering of blue wavelengths by atmospheric molecules. And this means that the light is much bluer in shaded areas, where illumination comes only from the sky, than in areas reached by the light of direct sun.

Light sources can be codified according to their so-called colour temperature on the kelvin (k) scale. Temperature is the mode of measurement because a heated object, such as an iron bar, will change colour from red through yellow and white to dazzling blue as the temperature increases. But remember that the kelvin number assigned to a light source relates to the colour of the light produced, not to the physical heat of the source. Thus, the colour temperature of daylight may be higher (because bluer) on a cold overcast day when all the light is coming from the sky, than in direct warm sun. At midday, average (photographic) daylight has a colour temperature of about 5,500k, and it is for light of this colour temperature that most colour films are balanced.

The colour temperature scale

Whether you are photographing in artificial or natural light, all light sources have a certain preponderance of wavelengths that give the lighting a particular colour. These different colours are shown below as a band of rising colour temperatures, extending from the reddish lighting characteristic of candlelight and sunsets up to the bluer light normally found in pictures taken in the shade or on overcast days. The colour effects of natural light in various conditions are illustrated above the colour temperature band, those of artificial light sources below the band.

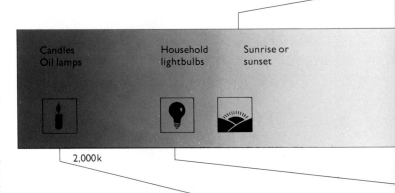

Candles
Oil lamps

Household
lightbulbs

Sunrise or
sunset

2,000k

Candlelight, in the absence of any other light source, produces a strong reddish-yellow cast, because a candle burns at a far lower temperature than the noonday sun. Although the light is usually too dim to show much detail, pictures taken by this source can have strong atmosphere, as in this shot of a Bangkok procession.

At sunrise and sunset, natural light is at its reddest because the light has to travel farther through the atmosphere. As a result, many short blue wavelengths are absorbed, allowing the longer red wavelengths to predominate. Below, the sunset sky has tinged the grey rocks of the Grand Canyon with red light.

At noon, with a few white clouds, daylight is neutral in colour. Because this is the light for which most films are balanced, the colours of objects under noon sunlight look correct. The picture of kites on a beach was taken in these conditions – and shows pure whites and reds in the nearest kite.

In the shade, photographs often have a strong blue cast, because objects are illuminated only by light reflected from the blue sky, and receive no direct sunlight. Overcast skies also usually produce bluish colours. Here, a cool blue light suffuses both the white ibis and the water.

| Morning or evening sunlight | Average noon daylight Electronic flash | Hazy sky | Heavily overcast sky | Reflection from clear blue sky (shade) |

5,500k   16,000k

Household bulbs burn hotter than candles, but produce a much yellower light than does the sun. This means that with ordinary daylight film in the camera, pictures taken in room lighting usually have an overall orange cast. The picture of a sleeping child shows that the warm effect of this light can suit skin tones.

Electronic flash is balanced to match the colour temperature of noon daylight. Thus, you can use it safely indoors or out, without creating colour casts. Had this studio flash portrait been taken by the light of tungsten photographic lamps, a special slide film (described overleaf) would have been needed.

Fluorescent light
This does not belong on the colour temperature scale because it is not a burning light source. The colour casts it produces vary greatly. Above, the greenish lights of an airport runway give the Concorde a surreal look.

115

The balance of colour/2

Not many situations in photography call for any special measures to cope with the colour quality of the light. Most pictures are taken outdoors by the light of the sky or sun, and slight variations in colour caused by weather conditions or time of day often add pictorial interest rather than cause problems (see pages 150-169). But sometimes a light source produces a colour mixture too far removed from the lighting for which your film is intended. When this happens, unacceptable colour casts may appear in the picture – for example, green flesh tones in a portrait. You can avoid this situation either by choosing special film or by using filters to modify the light as it enters the lens. Colour print films have a fair tolerance to different kinds of light because corrections can be made in processing, but with slide film the balance is crucial.

A special slide film is available for shooting indoors under tungsten bulbs. However, this film is balanced for powerful lamps used in photography studios, and will not entirely remove the unnatural colour cast produced by ordinary, lower-wattage bulbs. Alternatively, conversion and light-balancing filters are available in a complete range of colours, including those for fluorescent lighting. Some of the most useful filters are demonstrated here.

Daylight and film balance

Most colour films, print and slide, are designed to work best in daylight, accurately reproducing the colours we see (right). Almost all the film you use will be balanced for daylight. The exception is slide film balanced for tungsten lighting. This film has a bluer quality overall, rendering a scene lit by orange light from tungsten lamps as near white. Used in ordinary daylight, the film produces unnatural blues (far right).

1 – Daylight with daylight film

2 – with tungsten film

Tungsten light and film balance

In tungsten light, whether from ordinary bulbs or special tungsten photographic lamps, film balanced for daylight records an orange or yellow cast (right). Although the warm colour can be attractive, this is not how we see the scene. For more accurate results, the light can be partly corrected with a bluish No. 80A filter (far right, above). However, for greater accuracy, use slide film balanced for tungsten light (far right, below).

1 – Tungsten light with daylight film

2 – with No. 80A filter

3 – with tungsten film

Filtering fluorescent light

Although fluorescent lamps look white to the eye, they produce an unpredictable variety of colour casts on film – ranging through yellow, blue or green. The scene in an airport control tower at right has a distinctly greenish cast from the fluorescent tubes. A fluorescent filter (far right) does not balance the light perfectly to the daylight film, but does give a warmer, more natural look.

1 – Fluorescent light with daylight film

2 – with fluorescent filter

Filtering overcast daylight

Heavy clouds scatter the shorter blue wavelengths of sunlight, raising the colour temperature of the light and producing a blue cast on film (right). This still-life was rephotographed with a No. 81B pink filter to reduce the proportion of blue (far right). Many photographers use this filter as a matter of course on cloudy days.

1 – Overcast daylight with daylight film

2 – with No. 81B filter

Corrective printing: tungsten light

Filtration control in printing may restore accurate colours to print film. The portrait photographed in household tungsten light (right) has a strong orange cast. By asking the printer for a reprint with corrective filtration (far right), the photographer secured a much more accurate result.

1 – Tungsten light, uncorrected

2 – with corrective printing

Corrective printing: fluorescent light

The green cast from fluorescent light is more obtrusive than the orange from tungsten lamps. This portrait, shot by the light from fluorescent tubes in an office (right), has an unpleasant colour if uncorrected. When asked to compensate, the printer produced an improvement (far right), but has not succeeded in imitating the natural colours of a daylit scene.

1 – Fluorescent light, uncorrected

2 – with corrective printing

Choosing colour film

Most photographers simply want the film they use to record accurately the colours they see. Thus it may seem surprising that such a range of colour film is available. For 35mm cameras, there are several dozen types of daylight and indoor films. The reason for this diversity is that each film has its own characteristics, and you may want to choose different films for different purposes.

The initial choice, of course, lies between films for slides (transparencies) or for negatives from which you can make prints. Beyond this, a film's sensitivity to light is the main consideration. Fast films are very sensitive, and give the photographer great versatility, but slower, less sensitive films have other advantages. For example, they provide a good range of tones between light and dark. And because they make use of finer grains of light-sensitive silver salts to form an image, they can look sharper and are less grainy in big enlargements than photographs taken on faster film.

Although grain size is a consideration when choosing colour film, the film's colour rendition is often more important. A photograph of the same scene taken on different types of film will vary slightly but distinctly in colour, as the pictures below show. One film may record reds with special intensity. Another may distinguish more clearly colours that are closely similar. Yet another film may give the picture a warmer or cooler appearance overall – this is particularly noticeable in neutral colour areas such as black, white and grey, and in skin tones. In photographs, it is often in the skin tones that we are most sensitive to variations in colour values and most disturbed by unnaturalness.

Variations of colour are usually quite subtle, and are most obvious when you make comparisons between slide films; the printing process tends to reduce the differences between negative films. In general, photographers form their own preferences for colour film. The best way to make a choice is to try out a number of films, and decide which you like most. You may even want to use two different films, choosing for portraits a type that produces very natural skin tones, but preferring a different film for landscapes, where you may feel that the rendition of blues and greens is more important. The difference in the qualities of the blues is one of the features of the colour films shown below.

The colour characteristics of film
This garden still-life incorporates a wide range of colours. Shot on different types of film, the colours show slight but distinct differences – for example, in some the blue is stronger, in others the red. The green is particularly strong in the image second from right. However, there is no "best," because colour judgments are largely subjective.

Subtle colours and *flowing movement emphasize the grace and beauty of dance. Here, the photographer chose high-speed film to cope with the dim light of the rehearsal room. This film has helped to soften the colours.*

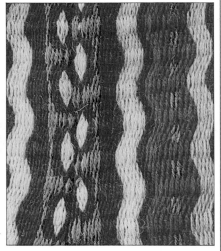

A vivid piece of woven fabric relies for its impact on the juxtaposition of primary colours. The photographer took the picture with slow transparency film, which has moderate contrast and good colour fidelity, suited to the reproduction of vibrant hues.

How colour film works

Colour print film is like a layer cake (above) made of gelatin containing grains of silver salts. Each layer records a different part of the visible spectrum – red, green or blue light. Processing creates a silver image where light was absorbed in each layer. At the same time, a dye image appears – in colour exactly opposite to the colour for which the layer is sensitized. For example, the blue-sensitive layer forms a yellow dye image. After bleach and fix have removed the silver image, the dye layers (visible in the magnified cross-section above) form the negative from which a positive print is made. Processing of colour slides is more complex because the film must form a positive picture. During processing, a second development introduces transparent dyes that form the image, subtracting appropriate colours from the light that passes through the slide.

Slide film

To achieve precision and brilliance of colour, many photographers prefer to use colour slide film – often called transparency or colour reversal film. Because this produces a positive film image directly, without an intermediate printing process, any adjustment the photographer makes to the camera's controls leads directly to a corresponding change in the appearance of the final picture.

Although colour slides need projection or enlargement to be seen properly, they display great brilliance and colour saturation. We see slides by transmitted, rather than reflected, light. Therefore, the range of brightness is higher – a slide usually has more snap than a print (see overleaf).

This impact derives partly from the higher contrast of slide films – they allow little latitude for over- or underexposure. On a dull day, or under flat lighting, this is an advantage, but on a bright sunny day, when the shadows are very dark and the highlights bright, high contrast can prove a problem. At worst you can lose highlight or shadow detail altogether, depending on how you set the exposure.

As a general rule, blank highlights – for example pale, washed-out features in a portrait – are more likely to spoil a picture than are murky shadows. For this reason, if you are uncertain about the light, some underexposure of colour slide film is better than overexposure.

Regular users of colour transparency film often deliberately underexpose all their pictures to take account of this – usually by a third or half a stop. Even in low or flat lighting conditions, slight underexposure leads to richer, more saturated colours. You can also underexpose by setting your camera's film speed control to a slightly higher speed – say ISO 80 if you are using ISO 64 film.

When the contrast between highlights and shadows is very high – in strong sunlight or when shooting into the sun – bracketing exposures increases the chance of getting just the picture you want. For the sunset pictures shown below, the photographer used this simple technique, making exposures at intervals of one stop above and below the setting indicated by the camera's meter.

The sunset looks different in this picture than in the three on the right, because the photographer varied or bracketed the exposure so that he could choose the best. The image above received two stops more exposure than the meter indicated. The result is pale but pleasing, with a satisfying balance of tones.

One stop overexposure gives the best balanced result. There is more detail in the sand spit and clouds compared with the pictures on the right.

Underexposure of colour slide film can add to colour saturation and avoid the burned-out appearance of sunlit highlights. For the picture of a flower bed (right), the photographer deliberately set the camera to give half a stop less exposure than the meter indicated. The inset shows the "correct" exposure setting (above).

At the metered setting, most of the cloud and sea areas are left as broad masses, but in compensation the red sky is particularly rich.

One stop underexposure produces an image that loses almost all the detail, but is still acceptable because of its dramatic effect.

Print film

While slide films have the advantage of brilliance and colour intensity, you need to project them onto a screen or use a small viewer to see them at their best. Many people prefer to see their pictures in the form of a print which they can hold in their hands. And because of the brilliance of the original, a paper print made from a transparency rarely seems as satisfactory. If your principal aim is prints, then colour negative film may be your best choice.

Because a print is viewed in different conditions to a slide, its colours may appear more muted, and some photographers prefer to work with colour negative film because they consider that the hues and tones of a print have more subtlety than those of a slide. Another significant difference is the low contrast of a negative compared with a slide. If you hold a negative up to the light it will look relatively dull. However, because the negative is only an intermediate step on the way to a print, low contrast is not the disadvantage it may seem. It means that negative film can be corrected for some over- or underexposure. As a result the film is ideal for

simple cameras that do not have sophisticated ways of avoiding exposure errors. Even when loaded into an SLR camera, negative film needs less care in assessing exposure than does slide film because to a certain extent exposure errors can be corrected during printing.

Printing a colour negative can be much more than just the mechanical process of reversing colours to their normal hues. First, a colour-correcting mask that gives the negative an orange tint has to be removed. Then, and more significantly, printing provides the opportunity to control selectively the overall or local colour of the picture, and to correct for errors in colour balance as well as exposure.

For the many photographers who print their own negatives in home darkrooms, the printing process can, in fact, be just as creative as actually taking photographs. Even if you do not have a home darkroom, you can exert some measure of control over the appearance of the final print by examining a contact sheet (see opposite) and giving appropriate directions to the colour laboratory.

*The **unreal hues** of a colour negative (right) are little help in judging the final colour of the print (above). Part of the problem is the orange dye mask that covers the whole of the negative. This helps to produce more accurate colours in the print, but makes interpretation of the reversed colours more difficult. The best general guide to how a negative will print is its density. A thin negative – one that is underexposed – has little visible detail and will produce a dark, muddy print. By comparison, a dense negative – one that is overexposed – creates fewer problems for the printer.*

Purple in the negative will appear as yellow in the print – the orange mask has combined with blue (the complementary of yellow) to give the purple appearance.

Yellow in the negative also forms its complementary colour – blue – on the print. The orange mask distorts yellow only slightly.

Green in the negative will print as red – the gloves in the girl's pocket.

A contact sheet, on which an entire roll of film has been printed, provides you with a convenient working guide to the appearance of all the pictures on the roll. Most laboratories can make a contact sheet, from which you can then choose which images to enlarge, say how they should be cropped to improve the composition, and decide if colour correction is needed. From this roll, the photographer picked out the image of the boat, and asked the printer to bring out the overall warm colour and crop the picture on the left-hand side. Both these changes would be simple to make in a home darkroom.

Instant-picture film

The obvious and spectacular advantage of an instant-picture camera is that it provides a finished print almost immediately. But apart from this fundamental attribute, an instant picture has a certain unique and identifiable quality – because the film reproduces colours by a method different from that used for any other type of film.

The elaborate chemistry of instant-picture film effectively packs a mini-darkroom into the sheet of film itself. Once development is complete, the image you see is the same size as the image recorded on the film, so that no quality is lost by enlargement. However, because the plastic-wrapped sandwich of film has to act as the print as well, the final image lacks some of the fineness of detail that can be achieved with conventional film. At the same time, the sealing of the actual print surface produces a slight diffusion of the colours. The combination of these two qualities gives the instant image its unique look. You will find that some subjects are actually flattered by the characteristic tonal and colour qualities of instant-picture prints.

In general, instant-picture film will give best results when the light is not too bright and contrasty, so that you can avoid the danger of colours being lost in inky shadows or pale highlights. The richness of the colours on the page opposite shows what can be achieved in more even lighting. Many of the newer instant-picture cameras reduce the problem of high contrast by providing automatic flash to lighten dense shadow areas caused by particularly bright sunlight.

One of the great attractions of instant-picture photography is that you can take advantage of the immediacy of the process by assessing results on the spot and using them as the basis for improvements. For example, the picture below was the best of several attempts to produce an image in which the moving ball stayed within the frame. In this sense, an instant-picture camera can be an invaluable tool for learning how to compose better pictures. No other kind of photography enables you to see so quickly and clearly how a three-dimensional scene will translate into a flat image.

The boy kicking a ball was the best of several shots. Because the photographer could see the results within a few seconds, he was able to take more pictures until he got the precise effect he desired, with the soccer ball included in the frame. The image appears sharp at the end of a trail of movement because the automatic flash of the camera fired to give extra light while the shutter was open. This froze part of the movement.

Instant pictures make an ideal visual notebook (right). On holiday, you can use them to make personal "wish you were here" messages to send to friends.

COMPOSING WITH COLOUR

Colour does more than bring photographs closer to reality. Particular colours often provoke strong responses in the viewer, creating tension or excitement, establishing a soothing feeling of equilibrium or jarring the senses. These powerful reactions may be independent of the subject of the picture, for we react to colour emotionally.

Controlling the strength or placement of colours can enable you to produce more effective colour pictures. On a few occasions you will have the opportunity to alter the colours of the subject – you could, for example, ask someone to wear a particular colour for a portrait, or change the colour of a backcloth. Much more easily, you can manipulate the colours that actually appear in the image by using techniques of composition outlined in the section that follows. For example, you can choose a viewpoint or a lens to include certain areas of colour and exclude others. You can fill the viewfinder frame with vivid hues, as in the picture here, or restrict bright colour to just a small area. And you can juxtapose two or more colours for either a calming or a vigorous effect. Colours create mood, and by using them in a controlled way you can give pictures just the impact or subtlety you want.

A sea of colour, created by the heads of innumerable wild flowers, sets up a lively and joyous mood. In this picture, close framing has concentrated attention on the interplay of the two colours, rather than the topographical details of the landscape.

127

Colour psychology

Individual responses to colour are highly subjective. But although most of us feel – rather than think – about colours, effective photographs often come from understanding the basic factors that influence people's reactions to colour.

Some reactions have a physiological basis. For example, yellow strikes us as lively partly because the cells of the retina are especially sensitive to yellow-green wavelengths of light. Some colour combinations appear vibrant because in looking at them our eyes have to make rapid adjustments between different wavelengths, whereas combinations of colours closer in wavelengths appear harmonious and restful. Again, bright, vivid colours – such as the red of the leaves in the picture at right – tend to seem nearer than do more muted hues.

More often, however, psychological factors are at work. These may arise from personal experiences, leading us to develop preferences for certain colours in clothes or furnishings. However, in learning how to use colour in photography, such personal reactions are less relevant than other responses to colour that are very widely shared – for example, the sense of warmth or coolness. Reds and oranges commonly seem to have an actual physical warmth, perhaps by association with fire and sun, whereas blue, by association with water, shade and dawn, seems cool. Another widespread feeling is that some colours are softer than others – pastel hues, such as pinks and pale greens, appear more delicate and gentle than pure, intense colours, such as yellows and reds, which can seem dramatic, strident, or even aggressive. By understanding such general reactions to colour, and by using one combination rather than another, you can consciously create a whole range of emotional effects.

Unbroken bands of cool blue convey a sense of peace and tranquillity. The atmosphere evoked by colours depends not only on their hue and brightness but also on how they are arranged – horizontal lines are much calmer in feeling than vertical or diagonal lines.

Bright red leaves *seem almost to leap from the page in this vivid image. Whereas bright, warm colours advance toward us, cooler, darker colours appear to recede. Here the muted background emphasizes the vibrancy of the leaves.*

The richness of colour

Strong colours have a more direct impact than those that are muted. Of course, many good photographs have soft colours, for these subtler hues often contribute to the sense of balance or atmosphere in a shot. But when you want colours to contribute drama or have a vigorous effect, you usually want them to appear at their most vivid.

The strongest colours are said to be fully "saturated" – a term borrowed from the dyeing industry. In photography, saturated colours are those that consist of one or two of the primary colours of light – red, green or blue – but not all three, because that introduces an element of greyness. At the same time the saturated colours look most vivid in a certain kind of lighting. For example, a pure red flower will appear more vivid than one that has a brownish tinge, but both will appear most colourful in light of medium intensity. Bright sunlight can make a colour

appear less vivid by lightening it – as the left-hand picture of the leaves below demonstrates. Shade, on the other hand, can make the colours appear darker.

When you have identified an area of colour that you want to emphasize, the following techniques may help you take full advantage of its richness. First, consider whether you can move around until the angle at which light strikes the subject brings out the strongest colour. Unless the subject reflects glare, a position with the sun behind the camera will usually be best. Second, to reproduce the colour at maximum saturation, take the exposure reading from the chosen part of the scene rather than the whole view. Although this may underexpose duller parts of the subject, the contrast can enhance the chosen colour area. Finally, with slide film, deliberately underexposing by a half-stop tends to enrich colour, as well as producing good shadow detail.

*1 – **Glare** reflecting from a shiny bush (above) gives the entire photograph a washed-out appearance. The other two pictures were taken in the same light, showing that colour saturation in direct sunlight depends on the lighting angle.*

*2 – **Backlighting**, with the bush between camera and sun, gives dramatic contrast in which the leaves are very bright. But because the light shining through the leaves is too strong, the colours appear somewhat washed-out.*

*3 – **Bright light without glare** shows fully saturated leaves. The photographer took up a position different from the first two, altering the angle between sun, subject and camera. Slight underexposure increases the richly coloured effect.*

Colour saturation
Pure colours lose intensity if they are either darkened or lightened. The saturated hues at the centre of the diagram are progressively desaturated by the addition of white or black. In photography, this means that colours lose strength in shade, or as light glares from a surface. Exposure errors also make colours look less vivid.

Low light mutes even the pure colours of these flowering trees, an effect that is increased by the haze. The green foliage is so dulled that it is almost grey in colour. In conditions such as these, only the strongest colours, perfectly exposed, will preserve any intensity.

Perfectly lit by soft window light, a bowl of fruit shows the richness of fully saturated colours. But even here, the effect of light reflecting from the subject can be seen in the highlights on the green apples. With slightly more exposure, these areas would have begun to appear too light and washed-out.

The importance of viewpoint

Colour in photography is more than just a property of the film you put into a camera. It can be the whole subject of the picture, the one element that makes a scene sing with energy. But like any other subject, colour has to be searched out and positioned carefully within the frame. For example, the photographer of the ruin in the picture on the right placed himself so that the sun could be seen forming rhythmic shafts across the great stone columns.

Colours do not have to be bright or spread across the picture area to be effective. In nature, it is more often a harmony of muted hues that gives us pleasure, or the single, vibrant accent of a flower or a tree in autumn flame. Yet a good way to start using colour as a subject in itself is to try to spot areas of plain, strong colour in man-made things — signs, shirts, dresses, boldly painted doors, fences, or walls (below) — and position yourself so that they fill the frame and make the picture on their own.

A row of beach huts makes a vivid, simple image that has all the more impact because yellow and blue are strongly contrasting colours. Together with the vivid blue sky, they turn the picture into an almost flat pattern of pure colour. The photographer had only to see the possibilities and frame the scene tightly.

The solidity, scale and romance *of the 12th-century Rievaulx Abbey, a ruin in North Yorkshire, are evoked here. The length of the nave is implied by the diagonal thrust of the architecture; the height fills the frame, yet the photographer, in choosing this moment, also shows this is a skeleton of a building, broken up by light and shade.*

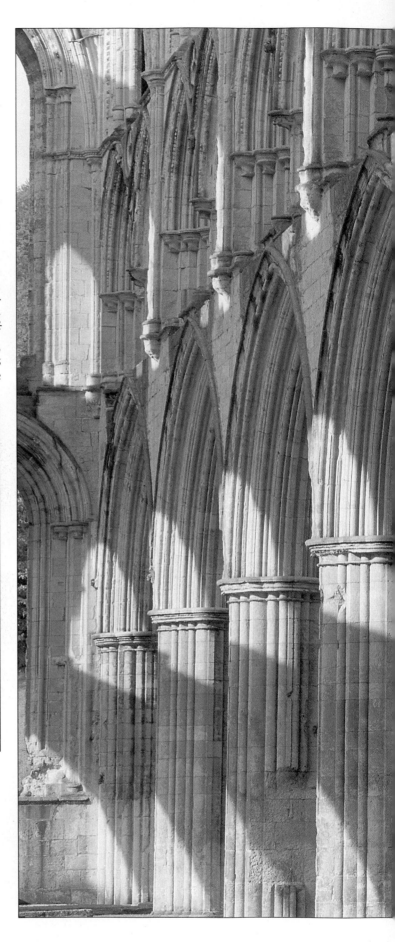

The colour accent

Colourful scenes make naturally colourful pictures, but much of our environment – particularly the concrete wasteland of modern cities – is drab. The weather, too, can have a profound effect on colour: snow blankets everything in purest white, and a scene that glows with colour in sunlight can look grey and forbidding in drizzle. Occasionally, a picture made up simply of subtle shades of grey has a quiet, pearly beauty of its own (see pages 138-139), but more often, a colourless scene looks simply dull.

Yet by introducing a single patch of colour into just such a picture, you can make the image pulse with energy, as in the picture of a dockside at top right. Even a small accent is enough to make a difference. For example, the graveyard on the oppo-

site page looks drab and depressing if you cover the flowers in the picture with your finger. But with the splash of yellow in the foreground, the picture springs to life as a harmonious image. The warmth of the yellow draws attention to other, more subtle patches of muted colour – the moss on the tombstones, for example.

The colours that best provide sharp accents are the warm ones – reds, yellows and fiery oranges. These colours jump out from the picture surface and command the viewer's attention. Cooler colours, such as blues and greens, often are less effective. Unless they are very bright and luminous, you may need to use them more liberally if you want to enliven a predominantly grey picture.

A fishing dock stands empty and silent as storm clouds sweep in from the sea. The heavily overcast sky had drained the sea of colour – but intensified the bright pink of a buoy – so the photographer stepped back to include this foreground accent.

This city square is full of activity and movement. The swarming pigeons fill the foreground, emphasizing the predominance of grey in the scene, so that the static, bold umbrella presents a double contrast. This vivid block of colour gives focus to the picture, drawing the eye to the centre and so to the face of the boy.

Yellow flowers in an improvised vase break up a drab pattern of tombstones. Because the stone slabs look so grey and ponderous, the blooms seem to glow with light and colour – whereas on a florist's stand, their brilliance might be lost among the other competing hues.

The dominant colour

The ability of modern colour film to reproduce all the brilliant colours around us tempts photographers to fill the viewing frame with the richest mixture possible. Sheer profusion of colour sometimes works well, but if you are not careful, the picture becomes a jumble of clashing hues.

Often, you can exploit rich, bright colour more simply by allowing just one powerful hue to dominate the image. Restricting the colour palette in this way can concentrate the impact of the picture – in the startingly blue seascape shown below, the single block of colour seems more emphatic than would several colours jostling for attention.

This way of using colour often works best when the dominant colour forms a unified background – as does the bright yellow of the umbrella on the right. The more intense the colour, the more it will dominate the image, but paler colour areas can be used to frame areas of the photograph that are a different hue. For example, in the picture on the right, the lemon of the umbrella makes a lively and vivid backdrop for the girl's shy smile.

To make best use of large, commanding areas of colour, try to set them off against other, more neutral, parts of the picture – here the black of the girl's hair, and her white shirt. You may be able to compose the picture so as to exclude discordant, distracting colour in favour of muted hues, such as the soft browns of earth – or of skin itself.

Sea and sky turn deep azure in dawn light. *The dark colour, deliberately underexposed, emphasizes the lights of the island temple.*

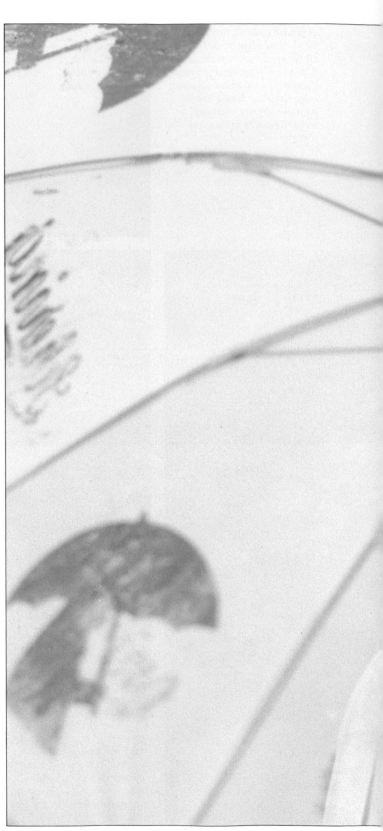

A row of beach huts at dusk creates a darkly harmonious colour composition. In spite of the fairly wide range of colours, the tones are all muted and therefore convey a sense of tranquillity. The cool blue sand in the foreground helps to unify the shot.

Half a lemon, dried out by the sun, rests on a translucent painted plate. Although the lighting is bright and direct, all three of the colours blend together, providing a simple but unusual example of warm colour harmony.

Dramatic colour

Just as some colours look balanced or harmonious when photographed together, others seem to contrast dramatically, and produce a bold, vibrant effect. You can use such dynamic combinations to inject excitement into a picture, to draw attention to a subject, or purely to create a strong abstract impact. Colour contrast is most striking when you restrict your picture to two or three colours – any more than this and the effect will be restless.

The colours likely to produce the most striking contrast are those that lie opposite one another on the colour wheel – the warm reds, yellows and oranges against the cool blues and greens, as in the photographs here. But what really determines how much two colours contrast is their relative brightness. Generally the effect is most dramatic if the two hues are equally bright. Pure colour contrasts are often easier to find on a relatively small scale – by closing in on a shop window display, for example. When you have complete control over the ingredients of your picture, you can consciously set up bold colour contrasts, as the photographer did for the fashion shot on the opposite page.

Ornamental plants *often have colours almost as vivid as the artificial dyes and pigments in fabric and paint. At left, richly coloured coleus leaves provide a perfect colour contrast – red and green are opposite each other on the colour wheel.*

A delicate green sapling *stands out crisply against the bright red fence, below left. The tree's fragility seems underlined by the strength of the red. A powerful yet very simple composition accentuates the dramatic contrast of colours.*

A bright blue door *makes the girl's yellow trousers look all the more vivid. The photographer has used the blue background to both isolate and frame the figure. And the picture shows how contrast increases when two light hues are juxtaposed.*

Restless colour

When a number of rich, bright colours crowd one another in a scene, the effect is usually lively, and the tone of the image upbeat. Such images are unusual in the natural world, because colours there tend to be muted or combine in a generally harmonious way. You are more likely to find bright arrays of clashing colours at carnivals, flower markets, amusement parks, or cities at night – places full of the things we make or display.

Although strong colours in themselves tend to give us pleasure – and we respond immediately to colourful views – photographing such scenes successfully can be surprisingly difficult. The challenge is to capture the vitality without introducing a sense of confusion. Our experience of the scene itself is different from the view of the camera because the eye is selective, and introduces order by concentrating on those elements we find appealing. However, when translated into a photograph, the coloured elements can assume equal importance and appear as a confused jumble. Even worse, the very profusion of colour can make individual hues lose their force.

Because we apply more critical visual interest to a photograph, we expect to find balance or a sense of coherent composition in the way the colours are arranged. To work, compositions with a restless array of colours must be particularly well planned.

The simplest technique for exploiting the vigour of clashing colours is to close in and fill the frame with their richness – as in the pictures here of a pile of plastic cups and a carpet of brilliant autumn leaves. Moving in is also a useful technique for organizing the picture when a situation bursts with life and movement – as might a carnival procession, for example. Multicoloured close-ups often provide a better sense of the excitement of the occasion than could a longer view. Try using a wide-angle lens.

Another way of achieving selection by framing closely is to use a telephoto lens from a greater distance. Do not be afraid to cut off parts of bodies or other elements with the edge of the frame. The lively night picture at the foot of the opposite page shows that you need only to concentrate on the pattern made by the colours in the viewfinder.

Plastic cups piled in a heap become almost overpowering when framed tightly to exclude the surroundings. Such synthetic colours often make brash, eye-catching images when seen together.

Fallen leaves form a pattern of russets, golds and reds. The colours of autumn sometimes seem subtle on the trees, but by raking them together and arranging them for the camera, the photographer exaggerated the contrasts and was able to produce an image with stronger colour opposites than those usually found in nature.

City lights jutting against the deep blue of the night sky here produce an exciting combination. The choice of an aggressive upward view contrasts the red and green of the traffic signals with the yellow of the floodlit church behind.

Using coloured foregrounds

To use colour creatively, you need to be able not only to choose colours that will work well together but also to control the position they occupy within the picture. Sometimes, a simple way of strengthening a composition is to use bold colour in the foreground. If the balance is right, this can act as a kind of frame for the scene beyond, leading the viewer's eye into the rest of the picture and perhaps establishing a colour key for the whole image.

Pure, bright colours create the most arresting effects. But you run the risk of overwhelming the rest of the picture if the foreground elements are too strong and sharply detailed. In the picture on the opposite page, the photographer overcame this problem by using a close viewpoint and a wide aperture to keep the bright lengths of material out of focus. When you want to retain detail in a coloured foreground, make sure that the area really strengthens the picture and does not prevent the viewer noticing important background elements. Compose the shots so that the proportions of colours, or their alignment, balance the composition, as in the pictures near right and below.

Colourful canvas stripes almost fill the whole frame, yet their receding lines lead us back to the hang-gliders in the distance. The photographer got down low to shoot across the wings of a grounded glider.

Shades of blue (below) link foreground and background in a picture that celebrates the power of pure colour. The crane, tilting in the opposite direction to the bar of the red sign, just balances the foreground.

Vivid bands of cloth hung to dry enliven this picture, even though they are out of focus. The eye hurdles them and passes on to the smiling face of the woman. The bold strength of the foreground colour balances the bright blue material in the background and together the two colour areas serve to frame the head – the only element in the picture that is in focus.

Using coloured backgrounds

Another important means of controlling colour combinations in photography is by carefully selecting the background. Provided the background does not swamp the subject but sets it off to advantage, you can often allow an intense colour to fill much of the frame. The subject itself will be emphasized if you choose a background that forms a strong contrast – a neutral tone for a brightly coloured subject, a vivid background for a more monochromatic one such as the limousine below. If you have total control, a useful technique is to place a light-toned subject against a darker background to increase the sense of depth – too bright a background will flatten the entire picture.

Background colours strongly influence the mood of a picture, dramatizing the image if the colour contrasts are vibrant, or suggesting tranquillity by colour harmonies. Remember that you can control the intensity of a background somewhat by using selective focus to soften colours. Outdoors, an eye-level viewpoint may give too busy a background. A low viewpoint will minimize the details in, say, an urban scene, emphasizing the expanse of the sky. Alternatively, simplify the background by getting higher. Sometimes a strong colour area, such as a sunset sky, can itself become the starting point for a picture and prompt you to search for a suitable subject to set against the background.

A golden brown wall, occupying three-quarters of the picture area, gives this informal portrait strength without overwhelming the man.

The brilliant red inspired the picture below. Realizing its background potential, the photographer waited until a strong subject arrived – the sleek, black limousine.

THE COLOURS OF LIGHT

Colours are inseparable from the nature of the light that reveals them. Although midday sunlight and electronic flash combine the colour spectrum in such a way that their light appears white, most natural or artificial light sources are tinged with colour. Some forms of street lighting even look bright green. Objects illuminated by coloured light sources are subtly transformed – an effect that is more noticeable in photographs than to the eye. If you take pictures of people when the sun is low in the sky, skin tones become warmer, whereas by the light of fluorescent lamps, faces may appear a ghostly shade of green.

Other qualities of light also affect the colours of objects in photographs. The direction and intensity of light determine the contrast in the scene, for example. And strong, direct light usually makes colours lighter, while more general, softly diffused light may actually produce purer and richer hues. Thus, the time of day and the weather strongly influence the colours in your pictures. Understanding these effects and identifying the colour of a particular light source will help you to exploit the full colour potential of the scene you are photographing. Certain lighting conditions also raise special problems of exposure. As a guide, captions to some pictures in the section that follows specify the film and shutter speeds, and the aperture size, for a difficult situation.

Rio by twilight reveals the variety of colours emanating from the many different light sources. Ebbing sky light reflects as blue on the water, while the last direct rays of the setting sun turn patches of cloud pink or orange. The city's fluorescent street lights shine green, with dots of orange from an occasional tungsten lamp.

Direct sun

Sunny days have pleasant associations for most of us, and not surprisingly, people take more pictures in sunshine than in any other kind of light. To some extent, the brightness and intensity of direct sunlight simplify photography, and give you extra flexibility. You can use small apertures for great depth of field, or fast shutter speeds to freeze movement. Alternatively, you can load the camera with slow film to take advantage of fine grain and detail. If this is coupled with a noonday shot, then colour accuracy is ensured because the light coming directly from a high sun is very close to white.

Making the most of the colours in the scene, however, may be unexpectedly difficult. Bright light can show colours in all their intensity – but only if the colours are perfectly exposed. The danger is that an area of bright colour – the red sail of a boat, for example – will be lighter than the surroundings, and will look washed out in the picture because you have exposed for the darker average tones. To overcome this, take the exposure reading from the colour area you want to look most brilliant, and if in doubt underexpose slightly – by a half stop or one stop. Sometimes, to show the strong colour at its best, you will have to accept underexposure elsewhere.

To prevent strong reflected light from washing out colours, use a polarizing filter. This will cut glare from shiny objects such as cars or other reflective surfaces such as water. The picture below shows how the same filter can also control over-intense light reflecting from the sky, giving you a strong blue in the upper part of the frame.

Photographing into the sun can be a frustrating affair; this picture shows the advantages of waiting for the right moment. The sun sits squarely in the centre of the column of cloud, a pleasing effect, and also a practical one as the cover diffuses the light so that glare is avoided with little loss of clarity in the scene.

In vivid red and yellow, a litter bin imposes a strong pattern of shapes and hues on a Florida beach scene. To darken the sky and make the bright colours of the hot plastic look deeper and richer, the photographer fitted a polarizing filter to the lens of his camera. When rotated to the correct orientation, such filters cut down glare and deepen the tone of areas of the sky that are away from the sun.

Low sun

Pictures lit by overhead sunlight conjure up impressions of hot, glittering afternoons, but the warm colours of low sun have more gentle connotations: morning light reminds us of the time just after dawn, when the sun's rays have yet to take the chill off the silent landscape. Sunset has a different, more romantic association – a lingering conclusion to a pleasant day.

Although our subjective impressions of morning and evening are quite different, these times of day are hard to tell apart on film. Low sun gives the same distinctive appearance to photographs taken early and late in the day. For a start, the raking light picks out textures and contours that are often masked when the sun is overhead. The long shadows are most obvious from above, so you can emphasize them by choosing a high viewpoint – as the photographer has done for the picture of the beach chairs on the opposite page.

The other distinctive characteristic of low sunlight is its colour. The sun's rays on their oblique path through the atmosphere pass through more dust and water than they do at midday, and this scatters the shorter, bluer wavelengths. The redder, warmer colours that reach the earth give a rosy glow to pictures taken by their light.

We accept the redness of sunset and sunrise as natural, and often attractive, as in the picture here of the little girl by the poolside. But colour film tends to over-accentuate the effect, and you may sometimes prefer to reduce the red tinge with a filter from the bluish Kodak No. 82 series.

Splashing in the pool at the end of a summer's day, this little girl is picked out in the warm colours of sunset. Far from needing correction, the reddish tones actually improve the picture. For a more formal portrait, or for subjects with a ruddy complexion, the warm cast might not be so flattering.

Drying paint on an artist's palette forms a pattern of colour and texture when photographed from above. The photographer turned the board until the low sunlight fell obliquely across it, picking out the shining whorls of pigment.

Early morning light has emphasized the pattern and colours of beach seats (below). The photographer rose at dawn to take advantage of the long shadows, and to avoid the crowds that would have marred the perfect precision of the picture.

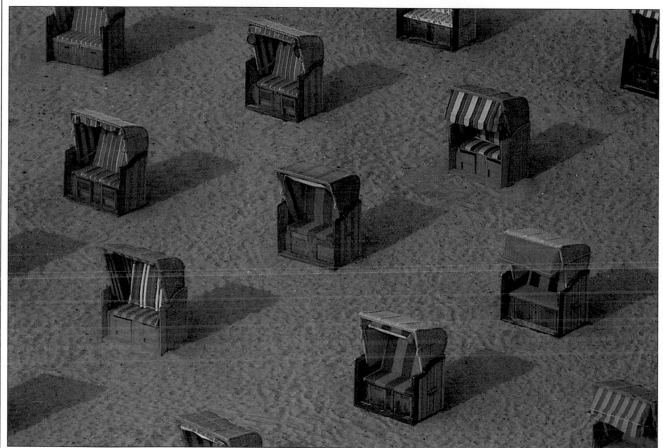

Backlight

The position of the sun always has a profound influence on the appearance of a photograph. But never so dramatically as when you point the camera directly toward the light source. This kind of lighting in a picture – usually called backlighting – works especially well with black-and-white film, because it produces highly graphic images that usually emphasize the outline and basic shape of subjects at the expense of surface texture, detail – and colour as well. Nevertheless, you can use the technique to take colour pictures of compelling simplicity.

If a subject is directly between the camera and the sun, the contrast range is likely to be so extreme that you will need either to overexpose the background or else to allow the shaded side of the subject – facing the lens – to become a dark silhouette. One exception is when the subject is transparent, allowing some light to pass through.

Because effective silhouette pictures in colour rely on the colour of the light source itself, morning and evening are the best time of day if you want to experiment. You may be able to use the warm, rich colours of sun and sky as the background. In the picture of the wooden pilings below, delicate pink light floods the whole picture as the water reflects the sky. To emphasize the subject's outline and retain the intensity of the background, take a meter reading directly from the sky, and perhaps increase the exposure indicated by one stop.

Although a silhouette is the normal effect of backlighting, the result is slightly different if the light source is just above or to one side of the subject. This produces a rim or halo around the subject, as in the picture of the girl below. You can make sure you retain the halo effect by taking a reading from the shadow area and then reducing exposure by two stops, and can experiment with the position and strength of the light to vary your effects.

Translucent subjects provide special opportunities for colourful backlit pictures. To capture the brilliant glow of the transmitted light, move in close and take a meter reading from the most important part of the subject – the petals of the yellow flowers, for example, in the picture opposite.

Outlined in sunlight, this window portrait would have been a silhouette but for the yellow light reflected from the girl's clothing. Look out for other similar reflecting surfaces to throw light into the shadows of a backlit picture.

Setting sun and high tide combine with mooring timbers in a spare, subtle image. By exposing for the background, the photographer reduced the seagull and its perch to their most basic and graphic outlines.

A vase of flowers glows with colour against the dark background of a walled city garden. By taking the picture against the light, the photographer used the delicate translucence of the tulip's petals to brighten the yellow.

Backlight/2

Some translucent objects, such as balloons, sails or umbrellas, take on particularly luminous colours when the sun is behind them. In a portrait silhouette such as the one on the opposite page, the light illuminating the balloons is being transmitted rather than reflected and the result is a picture that combines intense colour with emphatic shapes.

Transparent material placed between a backlit subject and the sun can also act as a natural filter – the girl's umbrella in the picture below has been used in this way, so that part of the silhouetted figure is softly and delicately lit. And unlike many backlit images, this picture has a full range of colours, intense in the umbrella and more subtle in the figure.

The coloured panels of an umbrella make a pleasing frame for a little girl's delicate features, and soften the strong sun behind her.

Bright balloons and red tape give an accent of strong colour to this dramatic image. The auras of light are produced by the lowness of the sun.

Diffused sunlight

You need to expose very carefully to bring out the brilliance of colours in direct sunlight, and to prevent them from becoming dissipated in glare and bouncing reflections. The pictures here show that colours often look richer in more diffused light. This is largely because contrast is reduced, making exposure easier to control. At the same time, the softer light helps to harmonize or balance colours – if that is your aim. And most important of all, diffused sunlight casts softer, less noticeable shadows. In portraiture, particularly, skin tones are thus recorded more accurately, and the whole image is less likely to be confused by the presence of deep, hard-edged shadows.

Light clouds and haze high in the sky diffuse light by redistributing the strongly directional rays of the sun across a larger part of the sky. The result is that shadows become less intense and their edges less sharp. Instead of being bright in the sun or dark in the shade, colours are brought closer together in tone. Provided the cloud cover is light, hues will retain their intensity. And, in the absence of hard shadows or reflected glare, the individual richness of the colours may actually increase. Because the key to showing any colour at full saturation is accurate exposure, the reduced contrast between naturally dark and light colours will allow you to choose an exposure that suits both. The varied greens of landscapes can thus be recorded with equal brilliance in the muted light. And in portraits, you can more easily blend and balance flesh tones, clothing and background colours.

A red fish, photographed in Kenya, glows with an almost unnatural brilliance against the equally vivid colours of the fisherman's shorts and T-shirt. The hazy sun reveals the full saturation of all the colours, without the intrusion of dark shadows. And the light keeps to a minimum the glare from the shiny scales.

Soft skin colours gave the key reading for this picture. But the sunlight, diffused by light clouds, restricted the range of tones. Thus reds and greens are correctly exposed also, and appear fully saturated. This light is ideal when you want to bring out the soft modelling of a face.

A sea of tulips vibrates with colour, every leaf, stalk and petal standing out in the soft light. Stronger sun might have made the flower heads gleam even more brightly, but the shadows created would have obscured the green parts of the plants, making them dark and underexposed on the film.

Haze, mist and fog

Photographs in dense haze, mist or fog produce some of the most delicate and subtle colour effects. These conditions not only weaken sunlight, but also spread the light around the subject, and themselves become part of the landscape. Haze is made up of microscopic particles suspended in the air — common during long, hot spells and also in polluted areas such as cities. The droplets of water that constitute mist and fog are larger and more often found at higher altitudes, or near rivers, lakes, or the sea.

Haze, mist and fog all thicken the atmosphere, acting as a kind of continuous filter. The result is that intense hues are muted to pastel. At the same time, colours tend to merge into a narrower range, creating images as beautiful and fragile as the harvesting scene below. In extremely dense mist or fog, the colours of a landscape may become almost monochromatic; hence the effects of these weather conditions can be useful if you want to give a soft overall tone to an image or to harmonize colours that would jar with each other in brighter, more direct light. And the absence of distracting detail can help you to appreciate the compositional qualities of a landscape more easily.

The softening of colour in haze, mist or fog becomes more pronounced with distance. The farther the subject is from the camera, the more simplified and delicate the image becomes, so that in a misty landscape, the different parts of the scene often appear to be arranged in receding layers of lighter and lighter colour, as in the picture of mountain ranges opposite. Sometimes, you can emphasize the sense of depth this produces by choosing a viewpoint that includes strong foreground colours.

Remember that the effect of fog and mist are not always regular and predictable. In a breeze, wisps of mist trail around trees, rocks and hillsides, often linking hues or emphasizing the colours of clear areas. And in dense but localized mist, of the kind that often hangs over wetlands early on a summer morning, trees and other subjects can appear almost in silhouette if the sun is directly behind them. Light itself then supplies the only colour, and in low sun, the scene may appear in delicate tones of orange or pink. You should look out for such unusual effects and exploit them by experimenting with viewpoint and camera angle. They open up marvellous opportunities for mood and atmosphere.

Late afternoon haze makes
this Burmese agricultural
scene almost monochromatic,
turning everything a warm
golden colour. The stubble
of the field enhances the
feeling of shimmering heat,
and the pale rim of light
around the group reveals a
perfect choice of exposure.

Receding mountains
are reduced here into broad
washes of colour by early
morning mist. This creates
an imposing sense of depth
as the planes of colour
fade from green to lighter
blues. The whole image is
given an ethereal quality
by the orange light tipping
the farthest ridges as the
sun penetrates the mist.

Rain and storm

Many photographers see bad weather as a sign to pack away the camera and go home. By doing so, you may miss opportunities for really exciting pictures. Dull, overcast lighting can certainly drain most of the colour from scenes and make everything seem drab. But often, light trapped beneath a lid of black rainclouds can give colours a dark, rich intensity never seen at other times. And although rain tends to soften and blur images, dampness often brings out subtle colours.

The spectacular brilliance of a thunderstorm, such as the one at far right, requires fast reactions – and, indeed, most storm-light effects are fleeting. The best chance of exploiting the vivid contrasts produced by a break in the clouds is to choose a high viewpoint. With a clear view over a wide area you can sometimes follow the bright trace of a shaft of sunlight moving across the landscape.

You do not have to wait until a storm is at its height to find dramatic light effects. A gathering storm can be equally impressive, especially in tropical climates, as the picture at bottom right shows. To preserve the relatively rich colours in the sunlight, and some sense of the impending darkness, be careful to avoid overexposure. You can emphasize the colour through contrast if you take a reading from the sunlit area, and then underexpose slightly to make the sky look still darker.

The picture below shows that the clouds which produce storm conditions may themselves form powerful aerial landscapes, especially if you photograph them from a distance with a wide-angle lens. The most exciting cloud formations of all are the tall, billowing thunderheads that form on hot afternoons in the tropics or in plains country such as the American Midwest.

The lowering blackness of the storm cloud gives this picture a power that seems all the more intense because the light is so muffled. The photographer waited until the cloud just covered the sinking sun, leaving shafts of light piercing through to gleam on the sea.

Raindrops *on a rose change its colour to paler pink against a background muted both by the rain and by selective focusing. Delicate colour effects can often be achieved just after a rain-storm, provided the light is good.*

Searing backlight *from an electrical storm produced this remarkable night shot of a train stopped on a bridge. The photographer put the shutter on a "B" setting for a time exposure that has captured several lightning flashes.*

Glowing light *bathes a landscape in South-East Asia moments before a grey sky releases a deluge of monsoon rain. In this rare and beautiful light, the contrast between light foreground and dark background heightens the colour.*

Dawn, dusk and night

Depending on climate, season and atmospheric conditions, the rising or setting sun can produce a remarkable range of flamboyant or subtle hues. At these times, the sky may be used as a richly coloured backdrop to a foreground city or landscape, or may provide sufficient pictorial interest to stand as a subject in its own right. Often, in order to bring out details of colours and cloud patterns in the sky, you will need to expose for the sky itself, leaving foreground elements to darken. With this in mind, try to choose objects in the foreground that will make strong silhouettes – or that have enough illumination of their own, as do the city buildings in the picture below right. A telephoto lens can emphasize the size and colour of a sinking or rising sun, or of the moon, when you want this to form the main subject, as in the photograph on the opposite page.

At dawn and dusk, it is not only the colours of sun and sky that vary from one moment to the next. The intensity of the light also changes rapidly. Therefore, keep rechecking your exposure reading every few minutes, and bracket exposures for safety. Because the light will be limited, if you are handholding the camera you will need a fast film, and a lens with a wide maximum aperture to allow a shutter speed fast enough to avoid the risk of camera shake. Often, time exposures are necessary, for which a tripod or other form of camera support is essential.

Cities at night are full of opportunities for colourful pictures – ranging from dramatic skylines to brilliant illuminated signs, multicoloured window displays, or the patterns of light made by moving traffic. Many of the most successful night pictures are in fact taken at dusk, when the sky retains some colour – and enough light for an exposure of perhaps 1/30 or 1/60 – yet street and domestic lights convey the impression of true night. In landscapes, the full moon itself can make an unusual light source for night-time colour shots. Contrary to popular belief, moonlight is white, not blue. Again, dusk is the best time for photographing the moon, because there will be enough light for a relatively short exposure. The moon moves more quickly than our eyes tell us, and if the exposure is longer than about a second, blur will begin to appear. In fact, the movement of the moon relative to the earth is such that it takes only about two minutes for the moon to cover the distance of its own diameter.

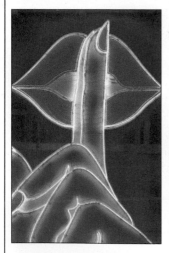

A neon sign, tightly framed, glows in luminous contrasting colours (above), emphasized by the use of daylight film. The exposure, with ISO 200 film was 1/60 at f/4.

Ablaze with colour, the radiant sunset sky creates a strangely surreal backdrop to the illuminated San Francisco skyline (ISO 400 film: 1/60 at f/5.6).

Pink light at dawn has tinted the distant mountain range, adding warmth to the cool blue of the sky and the snow. Dawn and dusk are marvellous times of day for shooting snow, seascapes, or any reflective subject that will pick up the colour of the light (ISO 200 film: 1/250 at f/8).

The full moon, through a 400mm lens, stands out from the blue evening sky. At twilight, when it has just risen, the moon seems to loom largest in the sky. Enough light remains in the sky to show the hill and trees in silhouette (ISO 64 film: 1/60 at f/11).

Snow

Winter snowfalls create some of the most exceptional scenery, with marvellous opportunities for crisp colour contrast. But you need skill to preserve both the pure whiteness of snow and its sparkling, crystalline texture. Calculating the right exposure is crucial – snow tends to look grey if underexposed, and featureless if overexposed.

The camera's meter will usually read from the highlights in snow, and indicate an exposure that compensates for the intense brightness. Thus, the result of following the meter reading may be a less brilliant picture than you want. To avoid this, open one stop more than the metered reading. If taking several pictures, bracket the exposures to make sure of at least one good result. Perhaps the ideal is an exposure that records the brightest areas of snow as fractionally less than pure white – darkened just enough to show a hint of texture.

The sparkle and crisp texture of snow are revealed best by sunlight from the side or from slightly in front of the camera. Being highly reflective, snow tends to pick up any surrounding colours, and especially the colours of the sky. This can produce beautiful effects early or late in the day when the light is pink or golden. In overcast conditions, a yellowish No. 81C filter helps to compensate for the overall blue cast. But on a clear day, when snow appears white in direct sunlight and a strong blue in shaded areas, you cannot use a filter without altering the purity of the white at the same time. If you are photographing mountain scenery, use an ultraviolet (UV) filter to cut down the overall blue cast caused by the scattered ultraviolet light at high altitudes. In order to enhance the deep blue of the sky, contrasting with the crisp white of the snow, you can use a polarizing filter.

Two skiers in packed snow provide warm colour against the coolness of white and blue. Using ISO 64 film, the meter reading was 1/500 at f/11, but the picture was taken at f/8 to retain the whiteness.

The golden light of a low sun early in the day bathes the snow with the warmth of the reflected colour. Notice how the slanting light glints on ice melting as the temperature rises.

Shaded foreground snow,
still reflecting blue light
from the upper sky, blends
softly with sky tinged by
the setting sun nearer the
horizon. Snow allows you to
make handheld exposures at
dusk even when little light
remains in the sky.

A latticework of snow
in a fence (below) creates a
pattern by breaking up the
bright colours of playing
children. Winter landscapes
are full of such opportunities.

Tungsten lighting/1

A Balinese girl looks out from a setting of carved splendour. Tungsten lighting used with tungsten-type film gives the scene a golden glow; daylight film would have made the tones warmer (ISO 160 film: 1/30 at f/2.8).

While most photographs are taken in daylight, opportunities for colour photographs of equal beauty and interest emerge when artificial light provides the main illumination. The most common form of artificial light for photography is flash, which has approximately the colour characteristics of daylight. Often, however, room or street lights provide sufficient illumination for a long exposure with a tripod – or they may appear in the picture as an inherent part of the subject. These lights usually have tungsten filaments, with a warmer colour than daylight, showing as orange on daylight film.

For convincing natural results, you may want to correct the orange cast back to normal by using the techniques described on pages 116-117. On the other hand, you may use the orange successfully to inject more colour into your pictures. As a general light source, tungsten provides an overall warm glow that is often attractive. In the same way, individual tungsten lights in a picture taken in very low light or darkness will show as points of orange or yellow light, enlivening the scene. Think about such colour effects before deciding that you need to use a conversion filter or a tungsten-balanced film.

Varied wooden surfaces create a rich interplay of tone and texture – the daylight film used records a delicate orange cast from tungsten room lights, producing an inviting feeling (ISO 64 daylight film: 1/2 at f/5.6).

Large cities are usually full of tungsten lighting at night, and even more so on festive occasions. The photograph on the left shows the Place de la Madeleine in Geneva, with a merry-go-round the centre of attraction. The overall feeling of warmth in the colours is characteristic of tungsten light recorded on daylight film (ISO 64 film: 1/8 at f/4).

A highway at night gives opportunities to photograph spectacular tungsten light effects. At right, two main sources create contrasting patterns, the regular lines of the lights acting as a foil to the curving trails left by car tail lights during a long exposure (ISO 64 film: 1 sec. at f/5.6).

Tungsten lighting/2

Mixed lighting is characteristic of many night-time photographs, particularly at dusk, when ebbing daylight may provide as much or more light than tungsten or other lights that have been switched on. While sometimes presenting tricky problems in terms of exposure or film choice, this kind of lighting also produces some of the most attractive colour effects. This is particularly true when one source of light predominates in the picture while another provides contrasting colour accents.

The basic rule for mixing tungsten and daylight is to decide which light source dominates, and choose a film balanced to that. Outdoors, just before nightfall, the main illumination comes usually from the daylight. On daylight film, the tungsten lights will appear orange, as in the pictures below. When there is less daylight than tungsten light, you could decide to use a conversion filter – or a slide film balanced for tungsten light – in order to show tungsten-lit colours more accurately.

The choice between daylight and tungsten light

film becomes more crucial for pictures of interiors in which you need to use a mixture of daylight and room lighting. If daylight from windows predominates, and particularly if the windows appear in the picture, there is no need to change from daylight film. The warm orange of tungsten room lights will add to the atmosphere, as in the interior scene on the opposite page.

In the early evening, or if the windows are small, the situation may be different, with the main light coming from the room lamps. To avoid everything turning orange, you should use a tungsten-light slide film – or a No. 80A blue conversion filter. Light from the windows will appear in the resulting picture as a shade of blue.

If you are undecided about whether daylight or tungsten dominates, always opt for daylight film. The warm glow of tungsten light exposed on this film is usually more acceptable than the cold blue of daylit subjects recorded on tungsten film, and looks closer to normal experience.

A streetlight glows in gathering dusk – daylight film records most of the scene in its true colors, but tints the lamp a warm orange (ISO 200 film: 1/30 at f/2).

The fish stall is lit by daylight, but the fish seller is lit by tungsten. On daylight film, his face looks orange (ISO 64 film: 1/60 at f/5.6).

A hotel lobby in Monte Carlo is lit by tungsten lamps, but daylight floods in through the glass doors. On daylight film, the tungsten-lit ceiling looks a rich orange, suiting the opulent decor. With tungsten light film or a colour filter, the ceiling would have appeared in true colours, but the entrance would have looked a chilly blue. The photographer rightly chose to use daylight film unfiltered (ISO 200 film: 1/125 at f/4).

A Palm Springs street is lit bright by tungsten shop lights of varying strengths. Here, the use of tungsten film adds interest by deepening the dusk sky (ISO 25 film: 2 secs at f/5.6)

Other artificial lighting/1

A tungsten lamp produces light by heating a thin coil of wire inside a glass bulb, but some other common light sources do not rely on heat. Fluorescent lights and other vapour lights such as sodium and mercury work instead by passing an electrical current through a gas- or vapour-filled tube. Light produced by the resulting spark nearly always has a distinctive colour – for example, sodium lighting, which is widely used on roads and industrial premises, is yellow. Sometimes the colour of vapour lights gives visual interest to scenes that might otherwise look mundane. But when you are using vapour lighting to illuminate other subjects – especially people – the colour cast may simply look wrong.

Sodium and mercury vapour lighting produces effects on daylight film similar to those produced by tungsten lights, but the colour casts cannot be eliminated in the same way. Whereas the light wavelengths of tungsten lamps range across the whole spectrum – but with a bias towards red – vapour lamps other than fluorescent tubes produce light of just one or two colours. Putting a filter over a camera lens can only remove colours, not add them. Thus, although you can filter out the excess of red light from tungsten, you cannot put back the wavelengths missing from sodium or mercury light, whatever film or filter you use. The best thing to do is to accept the situation and make a virtue of the resulting colour. For example, all the pictures here were taken on daylight film. In portraiture, where usually natural skin tones are important, you can introduce another light source, such as electronic flash, to light the foreground and counteract the colour cast in the main area of the picture.

Fluorescent strip lamps differ from other vapour lamps, because their glass tubes carry a coating of phosphors, which make the tube glow with light in a broad range of wavelengths. Although this produces a light that looks white, all but the most expensive lamps are deficient in red or magenta, and pictures taken by their light have a greenish tint. The actual shade of green depends on the type of tube and its age. If you are taking a picture in fluorescent light, and colour accuracy is important, you may need to make a series of exposures with different colour compensation filters. But generally, a CC 30M (magenta) filter, or a special "fluorescent to daylight" filter will help.

City streetlights usually are either sodium or mercury vapour lamps. In the picture above, the photographer used a long exposure with the camera on a tripod and took advantage of the striking colour of mercury lamps to turn roadside snow into a turquoise background for the lights of the passing cars *(ISO 200 film: 4secs at f/11)*.

A pool enclosure, lit by fluorescent tubes, seems to be suffused with green light. The colour is seen most clearly where the lights shine directly onto the blue-grey wall. The effect produced is one of subterranean chill and eeriness *(ISO 100 film: 1/60 at f/5.6)*.

The Jefferson Memorial
(above) appears the yellow
colour of its floodlights. To the
eye, the building would have
appeared much whiter, but
complete colour correction is
not necessary to achieve an
effective picture (ISO 400
film: 1/30 at f/2).

A statue in Brasilia glows
an unearthly green in the
light of mercury floodlights.
Such monuments often look
at their best by night, when
the strange and upredictable
colours of their lights show
up strongly in photographs
(ISO 200 film: 1/8 at f/5.6).

175

Other artificial lighting/2

In most twilight or night views of cities, every type of light vies for attention, producing a variety of lurid colours on film. Confronted with such colour bonanzas, there is little point in attempting to balance the film to the light. Daylight film without filters will show greens, yellows or blues from vapour lamps, red or orange from tungsten, and the pulsing colours of neon lights – all mingled with whatever varied hues the last rays of the sun create in the atmosphere. The effects can be spectacular, and the shot on the right shows just the kind of drama a mixture of colours can create.

Occasionally you will be able to exploit these possibilities in a more controlled way. If you remember that vapour light is likely to produce a strong colour cast on daylight film, you can contrast illuminated objects with the entirely different colours of the sky behind – as in the picture of a parked car below, which would have looked much less remarkable in ordinary lighting conditions.

*Multiple light **sources** illuminate this remarkable Art Deco London building in the early evening. Street lamps vie with lights on and in the building, producing a range of white and yellow glowing effects. The archetypal symbol of the city at night – streaks of amber and red trails from passing cars – complete the scene.*

A beach-side parking lot shines with the luminous green of fluorescent strip-lighting. Against the deep pink of the twilight sky, car and blank concrete take on an eerie starkness. Although the artificial light looked white to the eye, the photographer anticipated the more striking colour that film would show.

Flames

The light of flames from burning candles or oil lamps, matches or fires provides the most natural form of illumination other than daylight. Although light is unpredictable, flames create such atmospheric images that pictures lit by this source can be enormously rewarding. Most flames burn at far lower temperatures than do indoor lights and so produce light of a distinctly orange, even red, colour. Photographed on tungsten-balanced film, flame-lit scenes look a natural pale orange and on daylight film, which was used for all the pictures on these two pages, the warmer orange cast still looks acceptable, because even our eyes generally perceive flames as red or orange.

If you are taking pictures of only the flames themselves, accurate exposure is not particularly important – overexposed flames still appear yellowish while underexposure simply intensifies the red. Such moving flames as sparks or fireworks look attractive both when frozen by a fast shutter speed or when allowed to trace streaks of light during a time exposure. Choosing an exposure to record both the bright flames and the subjects they dimly illuminate is more of a problem. Place the subject as near as possible to the flame to minimize the brightness range. And read exposure from the subject, allowing the flames to be overexposed if necessary. You are likely to need fairly slow shutter speeds, even with high-speed ISO 400 film, and because exposure will be difficult to measure accurately, bracket your shots. Do not be tempted to supplement the light – using flash to photograph people around a campfire, for example, can destroy the entire mood of the scene.

A blacksmith, his face glowing red in the light from the fire, forges a horseshoe. *Daylight supplements the flames, providing the general illumination for the smithy (ISO 400 film: 1/30 at f/4).*

A row of houses, lit by a giant festival bonfire across the street, seems to be on fire as the flames reflect in the windows – an effect enhanced by the red light (ISO 200 film: 1/15 at f/2).

A glass of brandy, being warmed in a candle flame, makes an appealing still-life. *The orange light creates mood, but is barely strong enough for an effective exposure (ISO 400 film: 1/30 at f/2).*

A wood fire burns with orange flames in the snow. *The scene is lit entirely by daylight, giving a very slight blue tint because of the overcast sky. The winter's day, stark trees and black dress make a monochromatic, even colourless, image, brought to life by the glow of the fire (ISO 100 film: 1/125 at f/8).*

Fireworks burst orange and white over New York harbour, contrasting with the fluorescent green of the floodlit Statue of Liberty behind. Among burning light sources, fireworks are uniquely varied in colour (ISO 400 film: 1/30 at f/8).

USING COLOUR CREATIVELY

Most photography records the appearance of life, more or less unaltered by the imagination of the person who took the picture. In colour photography, basic techniques such as exposing correctly or matching the right film to the light source are used toward this end. But having understood that colour is attractive for its own sake, or has the power to move us, you may want to steer farther away from the literal representation of things. Often, by breaking the rules you can change the image that appears in the viewfinder and make a picture that will surprise the viewer – and perhaps yourself as well.

Some of the pictures on the following 19 pages show colours that are blurred, streaked by movement, or so isolated from their context by a close-range camera position that they make no literal sense. In others, reflections show subjects distorted beyond recognition. And in still others, filters have fragmented the colours of a scene, or introduced new and unearthly hues. Used skilfully, unorthodox techniques can allow you an artist's freedom to produce images of original beauty – patterns in which the colours do not define objects but serve your own creative purpose.

Condensation running down a window turns the image of the sun to the glittering texture of iced orange. Such a picture has no easily recognizable subject – our simple enjoyment of the colour is more than enough.

Colour and movement/1

Vigorous colours can add zing to action pictures frozen by fast shutter speeds – for example a ski racer in red angled against a wall of blue ice. Less obviously, perhaps, movement recorded with a slow shutter can produce colour effects of a unique and subtle kind. Colours blurred or streaked across the film have a lightness and fluidity all their own. And you can use movement to separate colours altogether from subject matter, and form abstract patterns of lines and swirls.

Some of the fun of streaking colour in a photograph lies in the uncertainty of the final image: you have to take some chances with this technique. However, you can exercise choice over the colours of subject and background, the speed and rhythm of movement, and the length of exposure – all of which have a bearing on the result. For the most dramatic results, choose a light coloured or illuminated subject with a dark background. The faster the subject is moving – and the slower the shutter speed – the more the colours will be diffused and streaked. Alternatively, you may be able to find a strong, static colour in the background and contrast this with a moving subject that is softly blurred.

Lines surging upward in a modern building (right) seem to pass through a descending figure. Having spotted the composition, the photographer set a slow shutter speed and waited for someone to arrive. The solid bars of colour in the background emphasize the muted hues and blurred shape of the dematerialized figure.

Deckchair canvases billowing in the breeze stream with fluid colours (above). The photographer used a wide aperture to obtain a shallow depth of field, so that only the middle chair is in focus.

A fairground in full swing throws out disembodied loops of coloured light against a deep night sky (below). The picture's drama comes from the brilliance and whirling motion of the subject, combined with the still, dark background.

Colour and movement/2

In addition to blurring moving subjects with a slow shutter speed, you can introduce streaks of light and colour into your picture by deliberately not keeping the camera steady. A long exposure will still be needed – perhaps 1/4 to a full second. Simply loosen your grip and move, shake or jar the camera during the exposure. Different movements will give smooth streaks, abrupt angles or graceful swirls. However, anticipating the final results can be difficult and you must be prepared to experiment.

Deliberate movement of the camera can be used with both static and moving subjects. If your subject is passing across the frame, you will need to pan the camera to follow the movement. At the same time, try giving a slight jerk or even twist of the camera. With luck, the subject will retain a recognizable shape but be surrounded by liquid colour, as in the picture of a jumping horse below.

An alternative way of breaking up the colours in a picture is to use a zoom lens and operate the zoom control during an exposure of about 1/4. The resulting effect of streaks radiating from the centre of the image can give a vivid impression of movement, even when the subject is stationary.

The lights of Hong Kong skyscrapers (above) shoot into darkness like exploding fireworks. From a height, the photographer focused on the buildings across the street, then changed the zoom setting of the lens during exposure.

A horse and rider clear a jump against a backdrop of swirling colour. Apart from following the movement of the horse with a panning technique, the photographer shook the camera to add fluid waves to the streaking.

White water bursts toward the camera as a kayak makes a difficult turn. Rather than using a fast shutter speed to freeze the movement, the photographer moved the zoom control during the exposure to increase the sense of energy.

185

Abstract colour/1

You can give your pictures a striking abstract quality quite easily by exploiting bold colour areas. All you need to do is to frame the subject so that colours rather than recognizable forms are emphasized.

A good way of making colour abstract is to exclude part of the subject. We identify things largely by their outlines and the context in which we find them. Isolated by tight or unconventional framing, objects appear as a two-dimensional arrangement in the picture. The effect of the yellow dress opposite was achieved in this way. By cropping out the girl's head with the frame, the photographer has removed the obvious centre of attention and concentrated on the composition as an arrangement of colours. Alternatively, you can tilt the camera so that the subject, seen from an unusual angle, becomes less important than the colours. You can even try taking the picture with the subject deliberately out of focus to make the shapes less distinct and more to be enjoyed as areas of colour.

Lighting is an important factor in emphasizing colour at the expense of literal representation. Flat light on an overcast day can be used to give a two-dimensional effect because there are no shadows to throw objects into relief. On the other hand, direct sunlight, provided there is no glare, can illuminate colours and bring out strong contrasts between them, producing strikingly vivid effects.

An inflatable play space provides the setting for a boldly abstract composition. The photographer framed the scene to balance the three strong colours of the translucent material and has excluded any details that could act as reference points to help interpret the subject.

A short yellow dress and tanned legs contrast effectively with the deep-blue background. Judicious framing cuts out recognizable features of the human subjects, transforming a fashion picture into an unusual abstract image.

Abstract colour/2

Colour patterns, formed by natural and manufactured objects alike, make fascinating subjects for abstract photographs. As with any abstract image, the key to a successful composition lies in framing to eliminate unwanted details.

Anything assembled in a series — panels in a fence, bridge girders, or a row of soldiers — forms a pattern, and tends to flatten the picture. Subjects containing strong lines and only a few bold colours make the most effective images. With an open pattern, the background can become part of the design; equally, an enclosed interior can produce a highly abstract effect without distractions.

A diagonal viewpoint often strengthens the sense of pattern — particularly if you use a telephoto lens. By giving an impression of foreshortening to the image, telephoto lenses produce pictures with a two-dimensional character — ideal when you want to emphasize patterns of colour — as the picture below of a military band demonstrates.

A military band makes a dense colour pattern dominated by the red and black of the soldiers' uniforms. From this distance, the ranks of guardsmen appear closer together than they really are — an effect that the photographer managed by using a 300mm telephoto lens to fill the frame with pattern.

The intricate repeated pattern on the ribs of this dome in Florence create an impressive web-like effect. The unusual viewpoint — most domes are viewed in profile from the outside — and the absence of clear clues disguises the identity of the feature. The bright light from the octagonal centre provides a focus, enhanced by the golden bands leading to each corner.

Finding colour in reflections

Reflections – found in all kinds of settings, indoors and outdoors – offer the photographer particularly unusual colour effects. Even a mirror gives back a subtly changed image of a coloured object, and less faithful reflective surfaces can make colours appear to flow, swirl or bend. Just a slight unevenness in a shiny surface – such as ripples on water – will alter and distort a reflection. The patina of time-worn brass, gold or tarnished silver will overlay a reflected image with added colour and texture. Chrome, a highly reflective surface, produces clear, bright images, but unusual effects are still possible because the curved chromework on cars and motor-cycles strongly distorts anything reflected.

Because colours are usually muted when ref-lected, you will get the most vivid effects in bright lighting. If morning or afternoon sun illuminates buildings on one side of a river, leaving the water in shade, reflections viewed from the opposite bank are far more intense than they are on a cloudy day, when the entire scene is uniformly lit. However, sometimes an effect depends on soft, diffuse lighting – as in the picture below, in which an expanse of still water echoes the soft colours of the scene.

To photograph reflections on a small surface, for which a close camera position is necessary, you can use a wide-angle lens or a small aperture to get sharpness in depth. Alternatively, focus only on the surface: the reflection will then appear as a blurred wash of colour. It might seem that the reflecting surface and the reflected image would always be equally in or out of focus, but for focusing purposes the image is farther away – light has to travel from the subject to reach the reflecting surface.

A lake mirrors the delicate hues of a pastoral landscape at sunrise (left). The glass-like surface of the water gives a reflection with only slight distortion, so that the effect is of a twin image.

A city street, slick after rain, reflects lights as a haze of colours (below left). By focusing on the surface of the road near the camera, the photographer has added to the soft, blurred effect.

A brass plaque in London adds its own mellow tones to the red reflection of a passing bus (below). The photographer focused on the plaque and waited for the bus to appear in view.

A small puddle beside a cobbled street reflects part of a sunlit building. Strong lighting and a well-judged angle give clarity and definition to the image.

Colour in close-up

Moving in extremely close can exclude distracting details and emphasize the strong colours to be found in relatively small parts of many subjects. You can even fill the picture area with patches of colour so tiny that they would normally go unnoticed. To move in very close you need special accessories, such as inexpensive supplementary lenses, a macro lens or a set of extension tubes. These allow you to achieve tight, graphic compositions in which the colours almost seem to leap out of the picture.

Manufactured items often contain strong dyes that are particularly vivid in isolated close-up. The little pencil sharpener below is an example of the way that, with careful composition, an ordinary object can take on a significance and interest that would never be evident to the eye. In nature, too, colourful subjects can benefit from close-up treatment. Few flower heads are big enough to fill the frame at a normal distance. But by moving in to concentrate on details rather than recording the overall appearance, you can isolate the vibrant relationship between colours or give emphasis to a rich single colour. The purple flower below would never have looked so pure and bright in colour had its full shape been included in the picture. The strongly three-dimensional shape of flowers can be difficult to keep in focus because of the limited depth of field in close-up photography. This is not a disadvantage when your aim is to exploit only one colour rather than to achieve the sharp clarity of botanical illustration. However, if you are photographing the intricate, multiple colour patterns of plants or insects, when the sharp edges of the colour areas are vital to the effect, you need to use an aperture small enough for the whole subject to be in focus.

A characteristic that is worth seeking out in nature is iridescence. The wings or carapaces of certain insects shine with a rainbow-like spectrum, which changes as the insect moves. Iridescence is also found in the feathers of some birds, perhaps most spectacularly in the peacock's, as shown in the photograph on the opposite page.

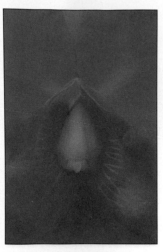

A butterfly wing (above) is seen as an intricate texture of scales when photographed at life size with a 50mm macro lens. Such close-ups of nature can reveal bold, even extraordinary, colour patterns and markings.

The vibrant petals of a flower fill the frame with richly saturated colour (above). Including only the centre of the bloom has restricted the colour range for a concentrated effect, achieved with a macro lens.

A red pencil sharpener contrasts startlingly with a green background (left). By closing in with an extension tube, the photographer made a strongly graphic picture from a small, everyday household object.

A peacock feather (right) shimmers with iridescence in a picture taken by fitting a supplementary close-up lens over a normal 50mm lens. The area of dark blue was carefully included to set off the shining lighter greens.

Special filters for colour/1

The most direct way of manipulating the colours of a photograph is to use a filter over the lens. Most filters are designed to make technical adjustments – for example, to match the light to the colour balance of the film in the camera. But many filters are now available that have a different purpose: to create dramatic images by altering the existing colours or by revealing hues that were hardly evident before.

The most basic filters of this type simply give the image an overall colour tinge. Pale-coloured filters have a subtle effect, modulating the colours in the scene and perhaps exaggerating a dominant hue. More strongly coloured filters can influence every part of the image, creating entirely new and even unrealistic colours. The shadow of the tree below has been bathed in lurid and mysterious colour by a deep green filter, making the picture look like a night shot even though it was taken in daylight.

Some coloured filters have only half their glass or plastic tinted, with a smooth transition from the colour to a clear part. Known as graduated filters or half filters, these can be rotated, allowing you to colour whichever section of the image you choose. In the photograph on page 95, one of these was used to tint the sky while leaving the rest of the image unchanged. In the photo at right, two graduated filters have coloured different parts of the image to add the colours of sunset to a daylight scene.

A tree's shadow falling on a rough stone wall made a strong and interesting image but one that lacked colour, so the photographer used a deep green filter. Daylight seems transformed into a strange artificial glow, with the green suffusing every part of the powerful image.

Pink and blue have been intensified in this simple beach scene by graduated filters – a magenta one rotated to tint the sky and a blue one colouring the lower part.

195

Special filters for colour/2

Some filters that have no colour in themselves can have dramatic effects on the way colours appear in photographs. Instead of modifying the colour of the light passing into the camera, they cause a controlled deterioration of the image. For example, diffusion or soft-focus filters use various kinds of mat surfaces to dull a picture's sharpness very slightly, so that details are obscured, as in the picture of flowers shown on page 95. Mist and fog filters change the image in a comparable way, but they have a much stronger effect. As their name suggests, they introduce a misty appearance, spreading out the colour of the bright parts of the picture. With an appropriate subject, this hazy look can add a nostalgic or

romantic feeling to your photographs – as in the picture of the girl in a landscape below.

Starburst and diffraction filters conjure up quite another mood – one of vibrancy and excitement. They are etched with varying patterns of grooves that can have different effects. A starburst filter creates a brilliant star from each bright point of light in the image. The number of points in each star depends on the filter. For example, in the picture of the neon sign at top right, the photographer used a two-point starburst filter. Diffraction filters go one step further: with surfaces covered by a complex grid of minute grooves, they split the rays of the star into a rainbow-like spectrum.

A girl in a landscape seems surrounded by a soft, hazy, almost dreamlike atmosphere, created by a mist filter that also spreads and emphasizes the pink of her dress.

Neon dancers gain extra sparkle from the grooves on a starburst filter (left), which caused the coloured lights in the picture to streak across the image as brightly ghosted lines.

A huge greenhouse gleams in the sun. The photographer used a diffraction filter to create coloured haloes around the points of light caused by the sun's reflection.

Special filters for colour/3

A multi-image attachment provides another, even more unusual, method of conveying movement on film. The little girl here was photographed with a Spiratone Motion Maker filter. This type of attachment is faceted so that part of the image of a moving subject is repeated. The photographer chose the girl's bright red coat and blue umbrella to form a strong colour contrast, and asked her to run across the dark asphalt. The result is a highly evocative image of damp and haste.

Special filters for colour/4

The dawn sky *(left)*, *silhouetting buildings and trees against its pale light, is turned into an image of excitement and colour by a prismatic filter. This produced displaced images of the sun and the silhouetted buildings, splitting the jagged horizon into rainbow colours and the sun into a brilliant spear of light.*

A city at night *(below) glitters with coloured lights, spread into streaks by a type of diffraction filter with a clear centre that leaves the middle unchanged. A slow shutter speed of 1 sec has blurred the tail-lights of passing cars.*

Glossary

The following glossary provides brief definitions of the technical terms used in this volume. It is intended primarily for quick reference, and most of the terms are explained more fully, and discussed in context, when they occur for the first time in the main text. You can find the relevant passages by referring to the index at the end of the book.

Accessory shoe
A fitting on top of a camera that incorporates a live contact for firing a flashgun. It makes contact between the flashgun and the shutter circuit to provide flash synchronization. The term "hot shoe" is sometimes used as an alternative to accessory shoe.

Aerial perspective
An effect of depth in a picture created by haze in the atmosphere, causing distant parts of a landscape to appear blue and softened.

Angle of view
The angle over which a lens accepts light or "sees". The longer the focal length of a lens, the narrower its angle of view will be – and vice versa.

Aperture
The opening in a lens that admits light. Except in very simple cameras, the aperture can be varied in size by a diaphragm, which regulates the amount of light passing through the lens on to the film.

Artificial light
Term used to describe any light source used in photography other than that from natural sources (usually the sun). Generally it refers to light specially set up by the photographer such as flash or floodlights. There is a difference in the sensitivity of photographic emulsions to daylight and artificial light, and films may be rated for either type.

ASA see FILM SPEED

Automatic exposure
A system that automatically sets correct exposure by linking a camera's exposure meter with the shutter or aperture or both. There are three main types: aperture priority (the most popular), when the photographer sets the aperture and the camera selects the appropriate speed; shutter priority, when the photographer chooses the speed and the camera sets the correct aperture; and programmed, when the camera sets both aperture and shutter speed. Aperture priority is advantageous when you want to control depth of field; shutter priority comes into its own particularly in action photography; and programmed exposure can be useful when the photographer has to react quickly.

Automatic focusing
A camera system that automatically brings the lens into sharp focus on the subject. The most common method of automatic focusing works on the same principle as the rangefinder, using two mirrors within the camera to compare two views of the same scene. Other systems use ultrasonic waves or a beam of infra-red light. The sound or light waves bounce back from the subject, enabling a receiver on the camera to calculate how far away the subject is and adjust the lens accordingly. This happens so quickly that to the photographer it seems instantaneous. Automatic focusing is used mainly on compact cameras, but autofocus lenses are available for some SLRs.

Available light
General term used to describe existing light, without the introduction of any supplementary light by the photographer. Usually it refers to low illumination levels, for example indoors or at night.

Backlighting
A form of lighting where the principal light source shines toward the camera, and lights the subject from behind. Because contrast tends to be high, judgement of exposure can be difficult in backlit scenes. An average exposure meter reading over the whole scene will often produce over- or underexposure, so it is advisable to take a separate reading for the part of the subject for which the normal exposure is required. As well as causing problems, backlighting can also be used creatively to give, for example, pure silhouetted shapes or a halo effect around a sitter's head in portraiture.

Bounce flash
A technique of softening the light from a flash source by directing it on to a ceiling, wall, board or similar reflective surface before it reaches the subject. The light is diffused at the reflecting surface, and there is a decrease in light power because of absorption there and because of the greater distance between light source and subject. Bounced flash is particularly used in portraiture, where direct flash is often harsh and unflattering and can cause "red-eye". If the reflecting surface is coloured, this will affect the light, so white surfaces should be used unless special colour effects are desired.

Bracketing
A way to ensure accurate exposure by taking several pictures of the same subject at slightly different exposure settings above and below (that is, bracketing) the presumed correct setting.

Cable release
A thin cable encased in a flexible plastic or metal tube, used to release the shutter when the camera is not being handheld. Use of the cable release helps to avoid vibration when the camera is mounted on a tripod or set on a steadying surface for a long exposure. One end of the cable screws into a socket in the camera, often within the shutter release button; the other end has a plunger which when depressed fires the shutter. Some models have locking collars, that hold the shutter open for long exposures. There is also a pneumatic type of release, operated by an air bulb and fitted with a long cable for remote control work, including self-portraiture. An air release is less liable to wear through friction, but will perish with age.

Cartridge
A plastic container of film that drops into the camera without any need for film threading. The film is wound from one spool to a second spool inside the cartridge. Cartridges are used mainly for 110 format cameras.

Cassette
A metal or plastic container of 35mm film with a tongue to be threaded to a rotating spool within the camera. After exposure the film is wound back into the cassette before the camera back is opened.

Cast
An overall tinge of a particular colour in a print or transparency. Colour casts often occur when the light source illuminating the subject of a photograph is not matched to the film.

Close-up lens (supplementary lens)
A simple one-element lens placed over a normal lens, in the same way as a screw-on filter, allowing the camera to be focused closer to a subject.

Colour correction filter
Comparatively weak colour filter used to correct for small differences between the colour temperature of the illumination used for a particular exposure and that for which the film was manufactured. An 85B filter is used with tungsten film in daylight, an 80A filter with daylight film in tungsten light. The name is also sometimes rather loosely used to describe the cyan, magenta and yellow filters that are used in an enlarger to balance the colour of prints made from colour negatives.

Colour negative (print) film
Film processed as a negative image from which positive prints can be made.

Colour reversal (slide) film
Film giving direct colour positives in the form of transparencies. It is also known as reversal film.

Colour temperature
Term describing the colour quality (particularly the redness or blueness) of the light source. The colour temperature scale is usually measured in kelvins (k).

Compact camera
A simple 35mm camera that has a non-interchangeable lens and is designed for easy portability, being intended primarily for taking snapshots.

Complementary colours
Two contrasting colours that produce an achromatic shade, white, grey or black, when mixed. Complementary colour pairs are important in colour films and printing processes. The pairs most commonly used are red-cyan, green-magenta and blue-yellow.

Cropping
Trimming an image along one or more of its edges to eliminate unnecessary parts, or framing a scene to leave out parts of the subject.

Daylight film
Film balanced to give accurate colours when exposed to a subject lit by daylight, that is to say when the colour temperature of the light source is around 5,500k. Daylight film is also suitable for use with electronic flash and blue flash bulbs.

Definition
The sharpness of detail and general clarity of a photograph. Definition depends on several factors – accurate focusing, the quality and resolving power of the lens and the speed of the film.

Depth of field
The zone of acceptable sharpness in a picture, extending in front of and behind the plane of the subject that is most precisely focused by the lens. You can control or exploit depth of field by varying three factors: the size of the aperture; the distance of the camera from the subject; and the focal length of the lens. If you decrease the size of the aperture, the depth of field increases; if you focus on a distant subject, depth of field will be greater than if you focus on a near subject; and if you fit a wide-angle lens to your camera, it will give you greater depth of field than a normal lens viewing the same scene. Many SLRs have a depth of field preview control – a button that closes the lens diaphragm to the aperture selected for an exposure so that the depth of field in the image can be checked on the viewing screen first.

Diaphragm
The part of the camera that governs the size of the aperture. The most common type is the iris diaphragm – a system of curved, overlapping metal blades that form a roughly circular opening that is variable in size, being similar to the iris of the human eye.

Diffused light
Light that has lost some of its intensity by being reflected or by passing through a translucent material. The translucent material can be natural (for example, clouds) or man-made (tracing paper). Diffusion softens light by scattering its rays, eliminating glare and harsh shadows, and is of great value in photography, notably in portraiture.

DIN see FILM SPEED

Disc camera
A pocket-sized camera that exposes a small circular disc of film contained in a light-tight cassette. Designed primarily for snapshots, the main advantage of the disc camera over types using conventional film is that it enables processing to be highly automated.

Element see LENS

Emulsion
The light-sensitive layer of a film. In black-and-white films the emulsion usually consists of very fine grains of silver halide suspended in gelatin, which blacken when exposed to light. The emulsion of colour films contains molecules of dyes in addition to the silver halides.

Expiry date
Date marked on film boxes to indicate the useful life of the emulsion. The date may be anything from 18 months after the time of manufacture for colour films to more than three years later for black-and-white films. In practice, a film may stay usable well beyond the given date, especially if refrigerated, but the manufacturer's recommendations should be followed. As films age, the fog level rises, speed falls and colour balance changes.

Exposure
The total amount of light allowed to pass through a lens to the film, as controlled by both aperture size and shutter speed. The exposure selected must be tailored to the film's sensitivity to light, indicated by the film speed rating. Hence overexposure means that too much light has created a slide or print that is too pale. Conversely, underexposure means that too little light has resulted in a dark image. Many cameras have built-in exposure meters that measure the intensity of light so as to determine the shutter and aperture settings that are most likely to produce an accurate exposure.

Exposure meter

Instrument for measuring the intensity of light so as to determine the shutter and aperture settings necessary to obtain correct exposure. Exposure meters may by built into the camera or be completely separate units. Separate meters may be able to measure the light falling on the subject (incident reading) as well as the light reflected by it (reflected reading); built-in meters measure only reflected light. Both types of meter may by capable of measuring light from a particular part of the subject (spot metering) as well as taking an overall reading.

Extension tubes

Accessories used in close-up photography consisting of metal tubes that can be fitted between the lens and the camera body, thus increasing the distance between the lens and the film. They are usually sold in sets of three and can be used in combination with one another, making possible a variety of different extension lengths.

Fast lens

A lens of wide maximum aperture, relative to its focal length, allowing maximum light into the camera in minimum time. The speed of a lens – its relative ability to take in light – is an important measure of its optical efficiency: fast lenses are harder to design and manufacture than slow lenses, and consequently cost more.

Fill-in light

Additional lighting used to supplement the principal light source and brighten shadows. In portrait photography, for example, a single light source, such as available light streaming through a window, might cast very heavy shadows on one side of the sitter's face. Fill-in light can be supplied by re-directing light with a card reflector or by using a flash unit, for example.

Film speed

A film's sensitivity to light, rated numerically so that it can be matched to the camera's exposure controls. The two most commonly used scales, ASA (American Standards Association) and DIN (Deutsche Industrie Norm), are now superseded by the system known as ISO (International Standards Organization). ASA 100 (21° DIN) is expressed as ISO 100/21° or simply ISO 100. A high numerical rating denotes a fast film, one that is highly sensitive to light (i.e. ideal in poor lighting conditions).

Filter

A thin sheet of glass, plastic or gelatin placed in front of the camera's lens to control or change the appearance of the picture. Some filters affect colour or tone; others can, for example, cut out unwanted reflections, help to reduce haze or can be used to create a variety of special effects.

Flash

A very brief but intense burst of artificial light, used in photography as a supplement or alternative to any existing light in a scene. Flash sources take various forms. Some small cameras have built-in flash, but for SLRs the most popular flash units slot into the top of the camera.

Fluorescent light see VAPOUR LAMP

F-number

The number resulting when the focal length of a lens is divided by the diameter of the aperture. A sequence of f-numbers, marked on the lens ring or dial that controls the size of the lens diaphragm, calibrates the aperture in regular steps (known as stops) between the minimum and maximum openings of the lens. The f-numbers generally follow a standard sequence, in such a way that the interval between one full stop and the next represents a halving or doubling in the image brightness. The f-numbers become progressively higher as the aperture is reduced to allow in less light.

Focal length

The distance, usually given in millimetres, between the optical centre of a lens and the point at which rays of light from objects at infinity are brought to focus. In general, the greater the focal length of a lens, the smaller and more magnified the part of the scene it includes in the picture frame. A normal lens for a 35mm camera typically has a focal length of 50mm, a wide-angle lens for the same camera one of 28mm, and a telephoto lens one of 135mm.

Focal plane

The plane on which the image of a subject is brought to focus behind a lens. To produce a sharp picture, the lens must be focused so that this place coincides with the plane on which the film sits in the camera – the film itself is the focal plane.

Focusing

Adjusting the distance between the lens and the film to form a sharp image of the subject on the film. The nearer the object you wish to focus on, the farther you have to move the lens from the film. On all but the most simple cameras, which have fixed lenses, you focus by moving the lens forwards or backwards by rotating a focusing control ring.

Format

The size or shape of a negative or print. The term usually refers to a particular film size, for example 35mm format, but in its most general sense can mean simply whether a picture is upright (vertical format) or longitudinal (horizontal format). Cameras are usually categorized by the format of the film they use.

Gelatin

Substance used as the binding agent for the grains of silver halide in photographic emulsions. Gelatin, which is also used to make filters, is an animal protein, for which completely satisfactory synthetic alternatives have not been devised. The properties that make it especially suitable for use in emulsions are transparency, flexibility, permeability by the solutions used in processing, the ease with which it can be converted from liquid to solid, and its protective bonding action towards silver halide grains.

Graduated filter

A filter in which a clear and coloured half gradually blend into each other. A graduated filter can be used, for example, to enliven a dull sky in a landscape photograph without affecting the rest of the image.

Grain

The granular texture appearing to some degree in all processed photographic materials. In black-and-white photographs the grains are minute particles of black metallic silver that constitute the dark areas of a photograph. In colour photographs the silver is removed chemically, but tiny blotches of dye retain the appearance of grain. The more sensitive – or faster – the film, the coarser the grain will be.

Highlights

Bright parts of the subject that appear as the densest areas on the negative and as the lightest areas in the final prints or transparencies.

Hot shoe see ACCESSORY SHOE

Incident light reading

A method of measuring the light that falls on a subject as distinct from the light that is reflected from it. To take this kind of reading, the exposure meter is pointed from the subject toward the camera.

ISO see FILM SPEED

Latitude

The ability of a film to record an image satisfactorily if exposure is not exactly correct. Black-and-white and colour print films have more latitude than colour transparency films, and fast films have greater latitude than slow ones.

Lens

An optical device made of glass or other transparent material that forms images by bending and focusing rays of light. A lens made of a single piece of glass cannot produce very sharp or exact images, so camera lenses are made up of a number of glass "elements" that cancel out each other's weaknesses and work together to give a sharp, true image. The size, curvature and positioning of the elements determine the focal length and angle of view of a lens.

Lens hood

Simple lens accessory, usually made of thin metal or rubber, used to shield the lens from light coming from areas outside the field of view. Such light is one of the sources of flare. Lens hoods are designed specifically to each focal length of lens, giving an angle of view slightly larger than the lens's. Obviously, a hood made for a long focal length lens would cut off the field of view of a wide-angle or standard lens, and as a general rule the shorter the focal length, the shallower the depth of the hood. Rectanglular hoods are more efficient than round ones.

Long-focus lens

A lens that includes a narrow view of the subject in the picture frame, making distant objects appear closer and magnified. Most long-focus lenses are of the type known as telephoto lenses. These have an optical construction that results in their being physically shorter than their focal length, and consequently easier to handle than non-telephoto long-focus lenses. In fact almost all long-focus lenses are now telephoto lenses, and the two terms tend to be used interchangeably.

Macro lens

Strictly defined, a lens capable of giving a 1:1 magnification ratio (a life-size image), but generally the term is used to describe any lens specifically designed to focus on subjects very near to the camera.

Motordrive

A battery-operated device that attaches to a camera and automatically advances the film and re-tensions the shutter after an exposure has been made. Some motordrives can advance the film at speeds of up to five frames per second, so they can be useful particularly for sports and other action photography.

Neutral density filter

A grey filter used to cut the amount of light entering the lens without affecting the colour balance.

Normal lens (standard lens)

A lens producing an image that is close to the way the eye sees the world in terms of scale, angle of view and perspective. For most SLRs the normal lens has a focal length of about 50mm.

Panning

A technique of moving the camera to follow the motion of a subject, used to convey the impression of speed or to freeze a moving subject at slower shutter speeds. Often, a relatively slow shutter speed is used to blur the background while panning keeps the moving object sharp.

Polarizing filter

A filter that changes the vibration pattern of the light passing thought it, used chiefly to remove unwanted reflections from a photographic image or to darken the blue of the sky.

Primary colours

Blue, green and red – the colours of light that when mixed together equally make white light, and that, when mixed in various combinations, can make any other colour. Saturated colours are "pure" colours that reflect only one or two primaries – when a third primary is introduced the colour is "de-saturated" toward white, grey or black.

Rangefinder

A device for measuring distance, used as a means of focusing on many cameras. The rangefinder works by displaying, from slightly different viewpoints, two images that must be superimposed or correctly aligned to give the exact focusing distance. A "coupled rangefinder" is one linked to the lens in such a way that when the two images in the viewfinder coincide, you know that the lens is automatically focused to the correct distance.

Reflector

Any surface capable of reflecting light, but in photography generally understood to mean sheets of white, grey or silvered card employed to reflect light into shadow areas. Lamp reflectors are generally dish-shaped mirrors, the lamp recessed into the concave interior, which points towards the subject. Studio electronic flash equipment is often combined with an umbrella reflector, usually silvered, mounted on a stand.

Reflex camera

A camera employing a mirror in the viewing system to reflect the image onto a viewing screen. The most popular type is the single lens reflex (SLR), which reflects the light from the same lens that is used to take the picture. The twin lens reflex (TLR) has an additional lens for viewing. A single lens reflex camera shows the image in the viewfinder as it will appear on the film, whatever the lens used.

Rim lighting

Lighting arrangement, principally used in portraiture, in which the light comes from behind or above the subject, creating a bright rim of light around the contours.

Saturated colours see PRIMARY COLOURS

Secondary colours

Colours resulting from mixing together any two of the primary colours, red, green or blue. The principle secondary colours used in colour film and printing processes are cyan (blue-green), magenta (red-blue) and yellow (red-green). The purity of these colours depends on their being produced by mixed coloured lights, and not pigments; red and green paints mixed together will not produce yellow, but grey, owing to the absorption of specific wavelengths of light by the pigment itself.

Self-timer
A device found on many cameras that delays the operation of the shutter, usually until about eight to ten seconds after the release is pressed. This allows the photographer to plan the picture, set up the camera and then pose in front of the lens.

Shutter
The camera mechanism that controls the duration of the exposure. There are two main types – between-the-lens shutters are built into the lens barrel close to the diaphragm; focal plane shutters are built into the camera body, slightly in front of the film.

Silver halide
A chemical compound of silver (usually silver bromide) used as the light-sensitive constituent in films. The invisible image produced when the halides are exposed to light is converted to metallic silver when the film is subsequently developed.

SLR see REFLEX CAMERA

Soft focus
Deliberately diffused or blurred definition of an image, often used to create a dreamy, romantic look in portraiture. Soft-focus effects are usually created with special lenses or filters embossed so that the glass surface breaks up the light by means of refraction.

Sprocket
A small projection on the camera spool that winds the film forward or back in the film chamber. The sprockets connect with the perforations ("sprocket holes") along the edges of the film, and move the film through the camera.

Standard lens see NORMAL LENS

Stop
A comparative measure of exposure. Each standard change of the shutter speed or aperture (for example, from 1/60 to 1/125 or from f/2.8 to f/4) represents a stop, and doubles or halves the light reaching the film. On some cameras you can make settings in between the standard marks – usually in half-stops.

Stop down
A colloquial term for reducing the aperture of the lens.

Subject
The person, object or scene recorded in the photograph.

Supplementary lens see CLOSE-UP LENS

Telephoto lens see LONG-FOCUS LENS

Time exposure
An exposure in which the shutter stays open for as long as the photographer keeps the shutter release depressed. Time exposures may be necessary in dim light and are usually made using a cable release and with the camera mounted on a tripod.

TLR see REFLEX CAMERA

Tripod
A three-legged camera support. The legs (usually collapsible) are hinged together at one end to a head to which the camera is attached. The use of a tripod ensures camera stability, particularly during long exposures.

TTL
An abbreviation for "through-the-lens," generally used to refer to exposure metering systems that read the intensity of light that has passed through the camera lens.

Tungsten light
A very common type of electric light for both domestic and photographic purposes – named after the filament of the metal tungsten through which the current passes. Tungsten light is much warmer (more orange) than daylight or electronic flash, and requires the use of a filter with daylight-balanced colour film to compensate for this and reproduce colours accurately. Alternatively, special tungsten-balanced film can be used.

Ultraviolet
A form of electromagnetic radiation close in wavelength to light. UV radiation is invisible to the human eye but can affect film, sometimes causing a blue cast unless removed by a filter.

UV filter
Filter used over the camera lens to absorb ultraviolet radiation, which is particularly prevalent on hazy days. As UV filters have no effect on the exposure, they are sometimes kept permanently in position to protect the lens from damage.

Vapour lamp
A lamp containing a gas or vapour that glows with light when an electric current passes through it. Mercury, neon and sodium vapour lamps produce strongly coloured light, but the light from fluorescent tubes approximates more closely to daylight.

Viewfinder
The window, screen or frame on a camera through which the photographer can see the area of a scene that will appear in the picture.

Wide-angle lens
A lens with a short focal length, thus including a wide view of the subject in the frame.

Zoom lens
A lens of variable focal length. For example, in an 80-200mm zoom lens, the focal length can be changed anywhere between the lower limit of 80mm and the upper of 200mm.

Index